Logic Design
A REVIEW OF THEORY AND PRACTICE

ACM MONOGRAPH SERIES

Published under the auspices of the Association for Computing Machinery Inc.

Editor ROBERT L. ASHENHURST *The University of Chicago*

A. FINERMAN (Ed.) University Education in Computing Science, 1968

A. GINZBURG Algebraic Theory of Automata, 1968

E. F. CODD Cellular Automata, 1968

G. ERNST AND A. NEWELL GPS: A Case Study in Generality and Problem Solving, 1969

M. A. GAVRILOV AND A. D. ZAKREVSKII (Eds.) LYaPAS: A Programming Language for Logic and Coding Algorithms, 1969

THEODOR D. STERLING, EDGAR A. BERING, JR., SEYMOUR V. POLLACK, AND HERBERT VAUGHAN, JR. (Eds.) Visual Prosthesis: The Interdisciplinary Dialogue, 1971

JOHN R. RICE (Ed.) Mathematical Software, 1971

ELLIOTT I. ORGANICK Computer System Organization: The B5700/B6700 Series, 1973

NEIL D. JONES Computability Theory: An Introduction, 1973

ARTO SALOMAA Formal Languages, 1973

HARVEY ABRAMSON Theory and Application of a Bottom-Up Syntax-Directed Translator, 1973

GLEN G. LANGDON, JR. Logic Design: A Review of Theory and Practice, 1974

In preparation

MONROE NEWBORN Computer Chess

Previously published and available from The Macmillan Company, New York City

V. KRYLOV Approximate Calculation of Integrals (Translated by A. H. Stroud), 1962

LOGIC DESIGN

A REVIEW OF THEORY AND PRACTICE

Glen G. Langdon, Jr.

IBM CORPORATION
SAN JOSE, CALIFORNIA

1974

ACADEMIC PRESS

New York   San Francisco   London

A Subsidiary of Harcourt Brace Jovanovich, Publishers

ACADEMIC PRESS, INC.
111 Fifth Avenue, New York, New York 10003

United Kingdom Edition published by
ACADEMIC PRESS, INC. (LONDON) LTD.
24/28 Oval Road, London NW1

Library of Congress Cataloging in Publication Data

Langdon, Glen G
    Logic design: a review of theory and practice.

    (ACM monograph series)
    Includes bibliographical references.
    1.   Logic circuits.   2.   Electronic digital com-
puters—Circuits.   I.   Title.   II.   Series: Association for Computing Machinery. ACM monograph series.
TK7888.4.L36   621.3819'58'35   73-18988
ISBN 0–12–436550–7

D 621.38.9'5835

LAN

Contents

Chapter 1 Switching Circuit Technology and Related Timing

Chapter 2 Theoretical Models and Synthesis Procedures

Chapter 3 Logic Design Practices

Chapter 4   **Interrelationships**

Preface

Our computer heritage is a rich and fascinating fabric of original thought. Many recent computer engineering graduates, however, are unaware not only of this heritage but also of current logic design practice. A present-day logic designer who ventures into the theoretical literature could become confused by the many types of circuits and the various modes of operation to be found. The disparity between theory and practice in logic design has not always been present; the pioneering computer engineers and theorists were often the same individuals.

One purpose of this work is to fill a gap in the computer design literature by concentrating on relationships dealing mainly with sequential machines. Thus this monograph is not for the newcomer; it is assumed that the reader is at least familiar with the material taught in an introductory switching theory course or a computer design course. Material covered in undergraduate electrical engineering courses is omitted. This work is to be viewed as reference or supplementary reading and should be of greatest interest to computer engineering educators and advanced students. In particular, it might advise students of that awakening many receive when they discover that the engineering aspects of "real" computer logic design are not what some (by no means all) textbooks may lead them to expect.

It is, unfortunately, not difficult to find examples of theorists revealing a lack of appreciation for "real" computer engineering practice. In a book on switching and automata theory, for example, one reads of the advantages of abstracting pertinent information from physical systems in order to deal with tractable mathematical models, so that a student would not find his new skills made obsolete by changing technologies. In the present study, we argue from the opposite viewpoint, emphasizing that the art/science of logic design is highly technology-dependent—far more so than the theorist may realize. The insights and benefits of thoroughly learning a technology and packaging scheme far outweigh the disadvantages. Although new technologies have come and gone, no new logic and timing schemes have been added to the technology-dependent logic and timing schemes of the first-generation computers. In addition, logic designers familiar with one technology can (and do) easily bridge the gap to another; and, in fact, they may influence decisions on selecting technologies to pursue.

To begin this study of theory and practice, we look back to the beginning of computer research. The best framework within which to examine the gap that has grown between theory and practice can be found in a review of the historical developments in computer logic design, switching circuit technology, and sequential machine theory. Thus, this review is divided into four chapters, three devoted to these areas and one that studies their interrelationships in the context of theory and practice and attempts to draw some conclusions.

Chapter 1 describes the development of the major technologies used to build computers. The evolution of switching circuit design is traced through three generations of technologies: vacuum tubes, discrete transistors, and integrated circuits. The striking feature about this development is the large variety of approaches that were tried. As might be expected, the designers' schemes for applying the technologies were also varied. A general familiarity with electronics is helpful in understanding this chapter.

Chapter 2 describes the major developments in switching theory that relate to logic design. In particular, sequential machine models and synthesis techniques (intended to be tools for the logic designer) are reviewed. This part of the review is not tutorial and an acquaintance with Boolean algebra is presumed.

Chapter 3 is a tutorial on logic design. An overview of the design process is presented; tools such as flow charts, design languages, and simulation are described. The important topic of system timing is also covered in this chapter.

In Chapter 4, the relationships between the theoretical and practical aspects of logic design are studied. We show the importance of the theoretical and mathematical models to be not so much in the direct design of digital systems, but in the supporting fields of fault detection and masking, digital simulation, and test generation. These fields are given ever-increasing emphasis since the advent of LSI; and thus we anticipate a fruitful future relationship between theory and practice in these areas.

Acknowledgments

For his encouragement and critical comments, the author thanks D. R. Daykin. He also thanks E. B. Eichelberger, K. A. Duke, and F. R. Moore for their interest and comments. C. K. Tang provided several useful insights. Discussions with S. Singh and J. G. Rudolph on this work have been very enlightening. The author has been particularly inspired by the recent accomplishments of C. Gordon Bell in bridging the gap between theory and practice. For his exposure to the theory, the author is indebted to T. W. Sze and M. K. Hu. For his initial exposure to logic design, the author is indebted to E. R. Taylor and J. A. Jaluvka. For his superb editorial efforts, the author is indebted to J. E. Riedy, and for bibliographic assistance the author thanks J. T. Dobransky. This work is dedicated to all those whose first experience with logic design was "chasing ones and zeros" through logic diagrams trying to figure out how some piece of logic ought to work.

Chapter 1

Switching Circuit Technology and Related Timing

R. K. Richards [1] has studied the theory of digital systems (taken to mean sequential switching circuit theory) within the context of digital systems and concluded that although the conceptual relationship to practice is close, the theory is not as useful as one might expect. We seek to understand why this has happened. A quote by Aristotle, brought to the author's attention by Mickle [2], suggests a starting point:

> Here and elsewhere we shall not obtain the best insight into things until we actually see them growing from the beginning.

In this chapter, we cover technologies, that is, the electrical devices out of which logic gates and memory elements (the logic designer's building blocks) are constructed. The aspects of the technologies, carrying over into the theory are the device behavior and the method of clocking or timing the memory elements. These aspects are illustrated by examples. We do not study the first generation technologies (vacuum tubes and relays) as such, but within the context of a particular computer, with the purpose of illustrating these aspects by example, and showing that the first generation computers gave rise to a large variety of logic and timing schemes which subsequent generations did not enlarge upon. As seen in the second and third generations, the selection of a particular logic and timing scheme depends upon the characteristics of the technology used. Certain of these schemes will be shown to have influenced the mathematical models of Chapter 2. In Chapter 3, we propose a classification of logic and timing schemes which encompasses all schemes encountered, we then address the question of the "adequacy " or completeness of sets of building blocks for sequential circuits. In the present chapter on technology, the foundations are laid for these aspects of the subsequent chapters.

A. Relay Technology

Bell Telephone Laboratories, the Computation Laboratory of Harvard University, and IBM built relay computing devices. The Harvard Mark I (or the automatic Sequence Controlled Calculator), designed by Harvard and built by IBM between 1939 and 1944, was a parallel, synchronous calculator. Counter wheels were used as storage devices, and a gear-connected mechanical system provided synchronism with a fundamental cycle of 300 milliseconds.

The Harvard Mark II, built by Harvard for the U.S. Navy between 1945 and 1947, used relays especially designed for the machine. Timing was provided by opening and closing pairs of contacts operated by a cam shaft rotating at one hertz. These were the only contacts that made (and, in general, broke) current; the current from the cam contacts passed through switching circuits whose contacts had already been set up. Some of the relays in the machine were mechanically latching; they possessed two stable states and had two operating coils. The timing cycle was divided into 30 steps, each timing contact being closed 16.67 milliseconds. The relay operation time was six to ten milliseconds so an adequate margin of safety was allowed. The use of timing signals emanating from a central source is a distinguishing feature of *synchronous* system timing.

While G. R. Stibitz was at Bell Telephone Laboratories he designed an adder using telephone relays. In 1938, S. B. Williams began designing a semiautomatic computer, called the Complex Computer (subsequently called Bell Model I); in 1940 it was demonstrated at Dartmouth College. The relay served as a memory element by connecting a normally open contact in a hold path with its own coil. When the relay was energized through an operate path, the normally open contact closed. This closed the hold path (providing other relay contacts in the hold path permitted it) so that the relay could remain energized after the original pick conditions went away. The relay was subsequently released by opening a contact in its hold path.

Six relay computers, Models I through VI, were built by Bell Telephone Laboratories; Model I used the excess-three code and slow release relays to measure the time required for addition. In Models II through VI the seven-bit biquinary code, which had a self-check property, was used at the suggestion of Stibitz. The "up-check" also (1) served as a completion signal for register transfers and additions, and (2) initiated the next operation. This type of system, which signals a *job completion* to initiate the next job or suboperation, is a distinguishing characteristic of an *asynchronous system*. This is the way that wide timing increments, required of the Harvard Mark II, were eliminated and the relays were permitted to proceed at their own speed.

B. Vacuum Tube Technology

The use of vacuum tubes in the distinguishing feature of the so-called *first generation* computers. Vacuum tubes found use as bistable memory elements for bit storage; one of the popular configurations was the cross-coupled Eccles–Jordon trigger circuit: a balanced circuit using matching tubes. Vacuum tubes were also used for logic circuits, generally in conjunction with diodes. One of the simplest ways to perform the Boolean operations of AND and OR is with diode resistor logic circuits as shown in Fig. 1.1,† along with the corresponding logic block. The 1-state is the high voltage level and the 0-state is the low voltage level. In Fig. 1.1a, all three input signals A, B and C must be at voltage level $+V$ *(logical 1) for output signal F* to be at the 1-state. If either A or B or C is at ground (0-state), then voltage $+V$ appears across resistor R, and output F is pulled down to ground, yielding an output of 0. The OR gate of Fig. 1.1b works similarly, except if either input signal is at $+V$, then the output signal F is at $+V$ or 1. As shown in Fig. 1.1c, AND gates may feed OR gates. The basic concepts of the diode logic gates have reappeared in technologies of subsequent generations.

Unfortunately, diode gates cannot be cascaded for too many levels before signal reamplification is required. An additional disadvantage is that diode circuits cannot be connected in a feedback loop without having amplification in each feedback path. With a load in the anode circuit, the vacuum tube provided amplification in each feedback path with logic signal inversion (or complementation). The cathode follower circuit was noninverting and provided current amplification.

1. First Generation Computers and Their Logic and Timing Configurations

This section will consider the early logic and timing configurations (i.e., the working of the memory elements and the timing of the basic machine cycle) of various first generation computers. The Electronic Numerical Integrator and Computer (ENIAC) will be described first since it is the

† The logic figure symbols generally conform to Standard ANSI Y32.14-1973, except for the OR, NOT, and Amplifier block symbol identification.

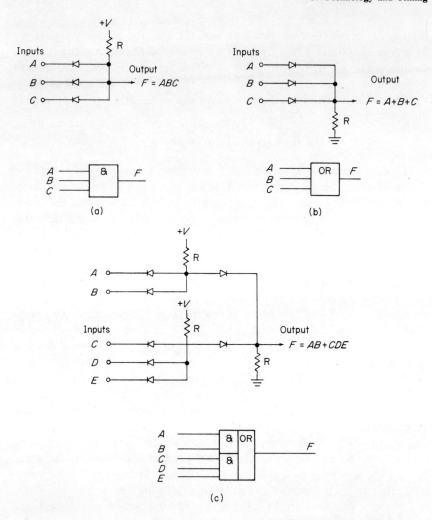

Fig. 1.1. Diode logic: (a) diode AND, (b) diode OR, (c) diode two-level AND–OR.

earliest electronic computer for which information is generally available. The other seven machines are mentioned in the order of the most synchronous in operation (the SEAC) to the least synchronous (the IAS computer). The machine classes selected for description are not exhaustive; however, each was selected to show a different logic and timing configuration.

a. ENIAC

The ENIAC was developed at the Moore School of Engineering at the University of Pennsylvania. It exclusively employed the standard counting and memory circuits of 1943 (such as were used in Geiger counters) because this approach involved a minimum of redesign [3]. Memory elements consisted of Eccles–Jordan *trigger* circuits; the basic concept of this circuit

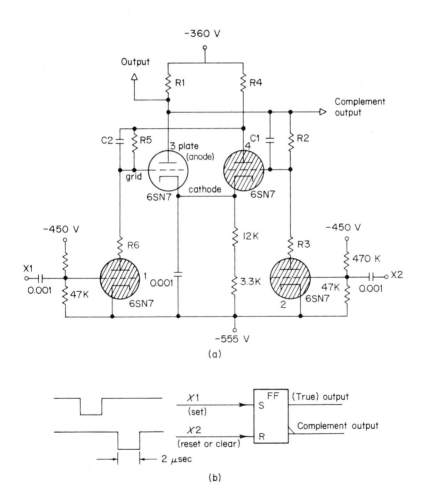

Fig. 1.2. The ENIAC flip-flop. (a) The Eccles–Jordan flip-flop circuit as implemented in the ENIAC. (Normally conducting tubes are shaded; resistor values are in ohms; R1 = R4 = 39K; R2 = R3 = R5 = R6 = 47K.) (b) The flip-flop logic block.

was cross-coupling two tubes to achieve two stable states [4]. When one tube was conducting, its attendant lower plate voltage was coupled to the grid of the second tube to hold the second tube from conducting.

When used by itself, as opposed to being a stage of a ring or binary counter, the ENIAC flip-flop took the form shown in Fig. 1.2. Tubes 3 and 4 formed the actual, cross-coupled, bistable pair; tubes 1 and 2 were triggering pulse amplifiers that increased the flip-flop operating speed. With tubes 1, 2, and 4 conducting, the circuit was ready for a set pulse (negative-going) on input X1. This pulse momentarily caused tube 1 not to conduct, providing a positive pulse to the grid of tube 3, which caused tube 3 to conduct, pulling current through plate resistor R1. The lowered plate voltage on tube 3 was coupled through capacitor C1 to the grid of tube 4, which caused tube 4 not to conduct. The circuit is ready for a pulse on X2 following the recovery time. The recovery time was determined by how long it took for the charge on capacitors C1 and C2 to stabilize following the "flipping" action. The flip-flops took 1 microsecond to change state and 4 microseconds to recover (i.e., be ready to receive the next pulse).

Note that there are other ways of operating or triggering the Eccles–Jordan flip-flop (see Williams [5] or Richards [6], for example). A notable variation is called the *JK flip-flop*. This flip-flop has two inputs, the *J* input behaves like a set input, and the *K* input is the reset input. However, when both the *J* or *K* inputs are pulsed simultaneously, the flip-flop toggles, i.e., changes to the other state.

The adder of the ENIAC used decade ring counters of 10 triggers each, and was ac coupled at the input, yet provided a dc voltage output. In the counter, only one trigger was set (i.e., in the 1-state). A signal pulse to a cathode reset all triggers or stages. In resetting the stage in the 0-state, the reset trigger gave a positive pulse to the next grid, which triggered the next stage to the 1-state. The pulse on the cathode had to be gone before the next triggering pulse occurred; otherwise the advance of the ring was opposed. This was a basic characteristic of *pulse-sensitive* memory elements.

Timing in the ENIAC was provided by a master oscillator operating at 100 kHz. The oscillator drove a 20-stage ring counter, which operated on the same principle as the decade counter. The resulting *machine cycle time*, or shortest period of time over which a sequence of events may repeat itself, was 200 microseconds. The oscillator pulse was 2 microseconds wide, and after passing through a delay to allow the ring counter outputs to settle, it was gated by gate tubes operated by the counter.

Since the flip-flops provided level outputs, the troubleshooter could stop or "single-cycle" the machine and determine the resultant state each time.

b. SEAC

The early computer industry used the pulse techniques that were developed for radar during World War II. The SEAC (Standards Eastern Automatic Computer; built by the National Bureau of Standards starting in May 1948 and dedicated in May 1950) was the first computer to make extensive use of ac or pulse techniques [7]. The storage or memory element was called a *dynamic flip-flop* [8]. It used a single tube driving a pulse transformer, whose output was fed back to the input through a delay circuit. The presence or absence of a circulating pulse indicated the storage of a 1 or 0 respectively.

In order to keep the circuits in synchronism, a clock pulse was distributed to every tube in the system. The clocking signals consisted of four phases† of a 1 MHz clipped sine wave; i.e., they were separated by 250 nanoseconds, called CP1, CP2, CP3, and CP4, respectively. Each AND gate had one of these signals as an input. A tube whose grid was fed by gates clocked by CP2 would normally be fed by a tube gated by CP1. In order to maintain the ouput pulse through CP2 after the incoming pulse had died, the output was fed back immediately and gated with CP2. This technique, called regenerative broadening, is shown in Fig. 1.3. (The block labeled AR signifies an amplifier.) The delay through the gates, amplifier, and output

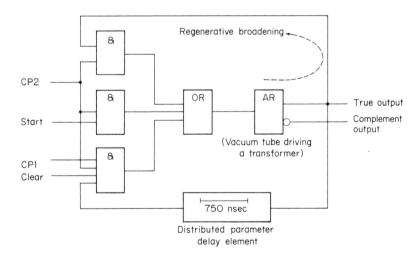

Fig. 1.3. SEAC dynamic flip-flop in typical configuration.

† The original design used three phases, but this was changed to four to improve timing tolerances.

transformer was about 250 nanoseconds. Therefore, for bit storage, the
feedback loop contained 750 nanoseconds of delay. To clear the flip-flop,
the feedback path was broken by a signal appearing at CP1 time labeled
CLEAR.† To effectively break the feedback, CP1 and CP2 (which overlapped) had to be AND gated to provide a narrow enough time increment to
be covered by CLEAR.

The SEAC made several contributions to computer technology. First, it
successfully used a building block concept. Second, information on the
SEAC design was readily available and had a strong influence on subsequent machines. It also influenced G. H. Mealy, who, in presenting his
model of a sequential circuit [9], assumed the mechanization of the
memory elements took the form of the clocked dynamic flip-flops (i.e., a
combinational circuit, followed by a delay which is fed back to the combinational circuit). This was the so-called *feedback delay model* of sequential switching circuits.

c. NORC, IBM 701, and IBM 704

The NORC (Naval Ordnance Research Calculator), built by IBM, was
started in 1951 and delivered in 1955. The IBM 701 and IBM 704 were installed in 1953 and 1956 respectively. All three of these computer systems
used the same family of logic circuits. The memory elements [10] used in
these computers are worth mentioning. They used a dual triode and were
logically similar to the SEAC dynamic flip-flop except the output was a
level and not a pulse. The output was delayed for one microsecond through
the Havens delay unit (designed by B. L. Havens) and then could be fed
back to the input where it was either recirculated or an external signal was

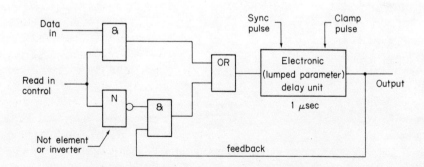

Fig. 1.4. The Havens delay unit in typical configuration.

† The overbar denotes logical negation.

read in (depending on the status of a control signal) [11]. The ubiquitous clock signal of the SEAC was not absent in the delay unit; a clamp pulse and a sync pulse were required. The circuit, shown in Fig. 1.4, uses a lumped parameter delay, in contrast to the distributed parameter delay of the SEAC, and did not have the 250-nanosecond delay and precise timing requirement of the SEAC. Inputs from other delay units operated from the same sync and clamp pulses had the proper timing.

The arithmetic section of the IBM 701 used these delay units for *registers*. A register was 36 bits (36 delay units) which were loaded and treated as a unit; 36 bits was the size of the binary number or word.

d. Whirlwind I and SAGE

Whirlwind I [12, 13] was built by the MIT Digital Computer Laboratory and put into operation in 1951. SAGE (Semi-Automatic Ground Environment) was a joint IBM and MIT Lincoln Lab design; the model was made operational in 1955 [14]. Many of the pulse circuits and techniques used in Whirlwind were adopted by SAGE.

The Whirlwind I master clock generated pulses of 1 MHz for the arithmetic unit and 2 MHz for other units. The pulses, 100 nanoseconds wide, were provided by a pulse tranformer and were used for triggering flip-flops; these flip-flops provided dc level outputs. The level outputs could be recombined with a clock pulse in a pentode gate tube called a gated pulse amplifier, where one grid input was a pulse signal and the other grid was used for a binary level signal. Combinational functions of flip-flop level outputs were accomplished by diode circuits. Thus, pulse and level signals were intermixed; on diagrams, the pulse interconnection lines used a triangular arrowhead, while the level signals used a diamond arrowhead.

The oscillator drove a distributor circuit which provided eight nonoverlapping clock pulses sent to the storage, arithmetic, and input–output (I/O) controls. These clock pulses were also AND-gated through the pentode gate tube with combinations of the 32, decoded, operation code signals to provide 120 timed signals which were used to control sequentially the execution of the operation (see Fig. 1.5). Figure 1.5 also illustrates the use of the "WIRE-OR" or "DOT-OR" function. When the anodes of two gate tubes were wired together to a common load resistor, a logical OR function resulted. Since its inception, the DOT-OR technique has played a very useful role for logic designers, and has carried over into transistor circuits where several transistors may share a common collector load resistor. The DOT-OR reduces gate count and delays. In most present-day technologies, this technique actually performs an AND function. Hence, it is also called DOT-AND or WIRE-AND, although the logic designer most often thinks of it as "or-gating" something.

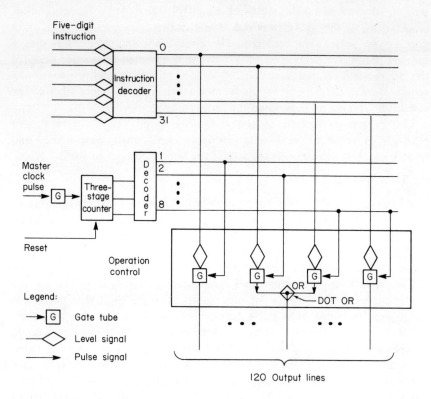

Fig. 1.5. Central control of the Whirlwind I.

In general, no overlapping of control operations existed. The control signal pulses, because of the amplification and reshaping by the pentode gate tubes, could pass through many cascaded gated pulse amplifiers, eventually controlling a flip-flop. For example, when a number in a register was added into the 16-bit accumulator, the interstage carry pulses rippled from the low order bits to the high order bits (a total of 16 stages) at their own speed.

The actual means of system timing, where the pulses could pass through a series of gated pulse amplifiers asynchronously is described by Richards [1]. The clock generated the time steps as a series of initiating pulses, which gave the synchronous aspect to the system, but the gated pulse amplifiers did not receive synchronization. The pulses propogated through them on their way to their eventual destination, usually a flip-flop.

The flip-flop was intentionally designed so that its output reacted slowly enough to the input pulse so that the previous flip-flop output could be gated with the same input pulse. This technique, which has no present-day counterpart, was known as pulse dodging and extensively used in the SAGE design; it permitted the clearing of a register with the same pulse that transferred its contents.

e. IBM 702 (and IBM 705)

The circuit family of the IBM 702 and IBM 705 computers was called a diode gate system by Richards [6]. Central to the system was a circuit, now often called a pedestal gate, shown in Fig. 1.6; it differentiated or converted an edge or change-of-level signal to a triggering pulse, and fed either the control grid of a tube or the base of a transistor. In this way the operation did not depend on the pulse width of the initiating change-of-level signal. Suppose the "Enable" level signal of Fig. 1.6 (identified by a diamond) is at 1 (a positive voltage), the "Transition in" input (identified by an arrow) at 1, and the "Pulse out" signal (identified by a triangle) is connected to a point near the reference, or ground voltage (0). (Usually it is this signal that feeds the control grid of a tube or the base of a transistor.) If the "Transition in" input changes to 0, then capacitor C discharges directly to ground through the diode, providing negative triggering current as shown. A positive-going signal at the "Transition in" input has a less dramatic effect because C charges up through resistor K. When the "Enable" signal is at ground (0), the diode is reverse biased and signal swings on the "Transition in" input has no triggering effect. A companion circuit to Fig. 1.6 for positive triggering pulses can be designed by interchanging the capacitor and diode (so the diode feeds "Pulse out") and placing "Pulse out" at a potential corresponding to a 1. An incoming positive-going change of levels yields a positive pulse out providing the pedestal gate is "enabled."

The state-of-the-art was advanced with this circuit (called a "Harper

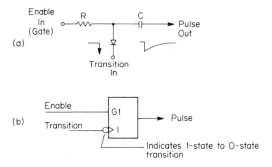

Fig. 1.6. The pedestal pulse gate. (a) Circuit. (b) Symbol.

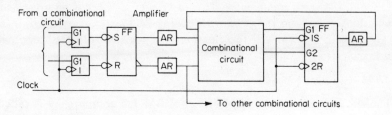

Fig. 1.7. The diode gate system of the IBM 702 and 705. (The pedestal gate is merged with the flip-flop for the right-hand flip-flop.)

gate" within IBM, after L. R. Harper) because it freed the system of the requirement to generate relatively narrow pulses and control their pulse widths, so this circuit has been used in vacuum tube and in transistor flip-flops. It is not commonly used in integrated circuits because of the cost of the capacitor. Memory elements that change state on a change-of-level instead of a pulse are called *edge-sensitive*. These flip-flops are also called transition-sensitive or edge-triggered.

In this circuit technology, the edge-sensitive, Eccles–Jordan trigger flip-flops provided level outputs which were passed through cathode followers for isolation and current amplification. The trigger outputs were fed to diode switching networks, which also included inverters. The switching network outputs provided the dc level gate conditioning (or enabling) signal. Clock pulses were fed to the diode input. An arrangement of the circuits in a system is shown in Fig. 1.7. All triggers were actuated by a clock pulse. Thus, time was divided into discrete intervals; the state of the triggers at the next interval was determined by the state of the triggers and primary inputs at the present interval.

f. IBM 650

The IBM 650, installed in 1954, used two tube circuits for logic: a cathode follower and an inverter. In addition, these two circuits were used for bit storage by providing a double inverter with cathode follower feedback. The circuit, called a *latch* [15], consisted of *direct-coupled* (d-c) combinational elements rather than ac input or pulse input flip-flops. Latches were used for storage (registers) as well as for timing rings.

The use of the dc (level-type) latch as opposed to the ac (pulse-type) triggered flip-flop was based on several factors. The proponents of the latch claimed it was insensitive to the noise problems inherent in a triggered flip-flop, due to unwanted triggering brought about by ac coupling from adjacent signal lines carrying pulses. Further, if pulse rise and fall times were not proper, the trigger might fail to respond. The latch responded only to dc levels which had to persist longer than noise pulses. Flip-flops such as

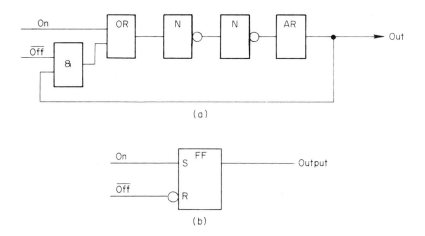

Fig. 1.8. The IBM 650 latch. (a) A latch as combinational elements. (b) A latch as a level-sensitive set-reset flip-flop.

this, which are dc-coupled and respond only to signal levels (as opposed to transitions or pulses) belong to a class called level-sensitive flip-flops. Figure 1.8 shows the latch (see Brooks and Iverson [16]) which basically was made from a diode AND, diode OR, and three tubes using dc level signals.

The latches could also be connected in a ring, but the plate of the second inverter was capacitively coupled to the grid of the second inverter of the next stage and the latch was no longer level-sensitive.

The IBM 650 used a magnetic drum for storage. The basic clock rate was 125 kHz, and three tracks on the drum were devoted to timing pulses, providing digit pulses, word pulses, and sector pulses. These pulses were counted by twelve-stage, ten-stage, and five-stage rings, respectively. The system timing has been characterized as synchronous in its fine timing such as a digit-by-digit clocked add operation, but asynchronous in gross timing such as when one instruction is completed and another program step is initiated.

g. NAREC

The NAREC (Navel Research Electronic Calculator) used some interesting circuits and system design techniques [17]. This machine mixes ac coupling with a basic level-sensitive flip-flop and an overall *job completion signalling* timing philosophy. The basic flip-flop circuit for bit storage is dc coupled as shown in Fig 1.9 in block diagram form. The actual circuit is something of an oddity. The input signals could come from

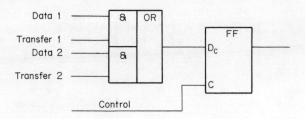

Fig. 1.9. Normal application of NAREC flip-flop.

a combinational switching circuit consisting of diode AND circuits, diode OR circuits, and inverter circuits. Today this type of level-sensitive flip-flop is called a *polarity hold* (PH), "sample and hold," or DC flip-flop. When the "Control" input (C) is in the 1-state, it passes the data input (D) to its output; and when "Control" is in the 0-state, it stores its previous output. The PH flip-flop is similar to the SEAC flip-flop and NORC flip-flop except here the output is fed back immediately, dispensing with the "unit" delay.

Several inputs could be OR gated together as shown in Fig. 1.9. The NAREC designers used this basic flip-flop circuit, together with appropriate capacitive coupling (triggering) and diode gating circuitry, to provide counting, stepping, and pulse-generating functions.

The various dynamic functions were performed by a compound circuit called an activator. Each activator output provided a control signal to perform one suboperation; for example, the transfer of digits from one register to another register. The completion of such a transfer was signaled by a comparator circuit. The completion signal was fed to an ac coupled amplifier driver which sent a special shift or triggering pulse simultaneously to all activators. The activator being reset would, by its change of state, send a trigger pulse through some combinational logic to trigger the next activator. The status of the control register and previous activator would determine the next activator. Thus, to perform the multiply operation, several activators were successively triggered. This circuit is often called *cycle controls* because it determines what the next cycle will be, based upon the present cycle (e.g., fetch, indirect address, add, multiply, etc.) and the possible status conditions. The cycle controls most resemble the model of a sequential machine.

h. IAS Computer

During the development of the ENIAC, many ideas on logic design were generated. In 1946 they were collected in a report by A. W. Burks, H. H.

Goldstine, and J. von Neumann called "Preliminary Discussion of the Logical Design of an Electronic Computer Instrument."† These principles of logic design were embodied in the IAS (Institute for Advanced Study) computer, built at the Institute for Advanced Study in Princeton, New Jersey. The engineering effort was directed by Julian H. Bigelow; two of his design disciplines were (a) "logical operations independent of signal waveforms" (i.e., no "pulses") and (b) "sequential control operation with each key operation initiated by the safe completion of the preceding operation" (a system control philosophy they termed "asynchronous") [18].

The designers of the IAS computer were not concerned with "part number proliferation," and did not use building blocks as such. For example, addition was done by a Kirchhoff adder which reduced eight possible input states to four voltage levels, and then subsequent circuits resolved the result to a 0-state or a 1-state. The flip-flop output values could be 0 or −20 V, whereas the gating control signals were +10 or −10 V.

The flip-flops, shown in Fig. 1.10, were dc coupled, provided level outputs, and behaved much like a flip-flop composed of two cross-coupled NOR or NAND gates [19]. To change the flip-flop to the set state, the

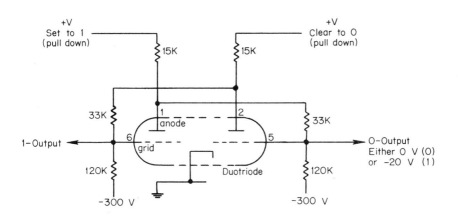

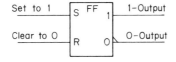

Fig. 1.10. The IAS computer dc flip-flop.

† Reprinted in *Datamation*, September 1962, pp. 24–31 and October 1962, pp. 36–41.

voltage on the plate or anode (pin 1) of the set side was lowered ("pulled down"), thus shutting off conduction. The plate voltage on the reset pin (pin 2) rose, was cross-coupled to the grid of the set side (pin 6), and caused the grid voltage on the set side to rise. This caused the set side to conduct. The output was intentionally taken off the grid because that was the last signal to change, ensuring the flip-flop had "turned over." Resetting was done similarly by pulling down the plate voltage on the reset side.

A notable feature of the IAS computer was the fact that it used double rank shifting registers, i.e., two flip-flops per bit; consisting of a lower rank or main register and an upper rank or temporary register. The lower rank could transfer bits to the upper rank only; whereas the upper rank could transfer to the lower rank either shifting one bit position right or shifting one bit position left. (Thus, in order to transfer a number unshifted from the upper rank to the lower rank, it was necessary to shift down left, gate up, and then shift down right—a maneuver called a zig-zag operation.) To perform a typical left shift of one bit, the upper rank flip-flops were all set to the 1-state. Then a control signal was AND gated with the complement output side of the lower rank flip-flops to reset the upper rank, if the lower rank contained a 0. This operation was called "gate up zeros." Then the lower rank flip-flops were all set to the 1-state, and the fourth and final suboperation was called "shift down left zeros."

The double rank binary counter [20, 21] of the IAS computer also used two flip-flops per bit; the lower rank held a "true" count and the upper rank held a "false" count. To count, a two-phase signal was applied, alternately initiating the "up" gates and "down" gates. The use of a secondary flip-flop to store the state of a primary flip-flop while it was changing was another design principle of J. H. Bigelow.

The IAS computer was controlled through completion signals to initiate the next operation. This type of system timing is called asynchronous. The completion signals for the phases of the shifting operation were derived from a prototype timing toggle. The completion signal for a ripple carry parallel addition was a 12-microsecond delay line signal. (A 40-stage carry ripple took 8–10 microseconds.) The only clock in the computer belonged to the memory and emitted a pulse every 24 microseconds. To access memory, a main control request signal was raised. At one point in the clock cycle the request line was sampled; if it received a request signal, then memory would immediately send an acknowledgement signal back to main control. When the requested information was placed in the memory register, a completion signal was sent to main control.

2. Summary of Early Computers

a. Logic and Timing Schemes

Many system timing schemes have been described; these used level signals in some cases, pulse signals in others, and sometimes a mixture of

TABLE 1.1. Logic and Timing Configurations of Several First Generation Computers

	Initiation/ Operational Dates	Basic Cycle Timing	Device Coupling Scheme	Type of Flip-Flop or Memory Element
ENIAC	1943/1946	20 stage ring counter provides basic timing cycle	Flip-flop and gate outputs dc coupled, ac coupled clock pulses	Eccles–Jordan pulse-sensitive flip-flops, level output
SEAC	1948/1950	Each gate timed by a clock signal from the four phase clock	ac coupled signals	Pulse-sensitive delay unit, pulse output (delay line model)
IBM 701	1950/1952	Every memory element is clocked	dc coupled logic signals, ac coupled clock signals	Pulse-sensitive delay unit, level output (delay line model)
Whirl-wind I	1947/1951	Clock pulse distributor provides 8 pulses each cycle	Mixed pulse and level signals, mixed in gated pulse amplifier	Clock pulses rippled through gates to switch pulse-sensitive, level output flip-flops
IBM 702	1951/1954	All memory elements clocked	dc coupled logic signals	Edge-sensitive Eccles–Jordan flip-flop, level output
IBM 650	1949/1953	Clocked by pulse-sensitive ring counter, level outputs	dc coupling except for ring counter	Level-sensitive, level output latch
NAREC	/1953	Timed by completion signal to ac coupled "actuator"	dc coupled except for actuator or counting circuits	Level-sensitive PH memory element, level output
IAS Computer	1946/1952	Timed by completion signal	Entirely dc coupled	Level-sensitive set-clear flip-flop, level output

the two. In the case of the IAS computer, the signals were all of the dc or level type, and all timing was done by completion signals. In the SEAC, the flip-flops were all pulse input and pulse output, and dc level signals did not appear. Clock pulse inputs and regenerative broadening provided retiming of the signals at each vacuum tube. The Whirlwind I circuits combined pulse and level signals in the pulse amplifier "gate tubes." This provided reshaping of the pulses, but clock pulses did not regulate every gate as they did in the SEAC. The Whirlwind I flip-flops were pulse input, level output. The IBM 650 generally used level signals and a dc-coupled latch for storage; but the system, unlike the IAS computer was nevertheless regulated by an ac-coupled timing ring. The NAREC flip-flop was direct-coupled and used completion signals to start the next operation, but the activators used triggering pulses. The two extremes of system timing were the fully clocked SEAC timing and the unclocked, completion signal oriented timing of the IAS computer. A summary of these schemes appears in Table 1.1.

b. The Circuit Families

The logic circuits described so far may be classified as decision (gate or combinational) elements performing AND, OR, NOT, or amplification functions, or memory elements performing a storage function. In the early literature, the AND was often called a *gate*, and the OR was called a buffer; today a gate is any combinational block and a buffer is usually a means to transmit data between two devices of dissimilar data rates. (Note that the term *gate* can also be used in trigger circuits like those in the Whirlwind I and Figure 1.6 where a level (gate) signal allows a dynamic signal (pulse) to pass.)

In general, a decision element may be defined as a basic logic block whose output, after perhaps a duration called the gate delay, is a Boolean function of its present state of input values (input state). There is a test to determine whether or not a logic building block exhibits the property of memory. If there is some input state for which there is more than one possible output state, the block has memory, i.e., it has more than one internal state upon which the output depends; several of the memory elements that have been described include:

(1) Eccles–Jordan flip-flop which responded to pulses,
(2) IAS computer flip-flop which responsed to dc level "pull-over" signals,
(3) SEAC dynamic flip-flop,
(4) NORC delay unit with a combinational circuit (followed by amplification and delayed one time unit) fed back until the flip-flop was to be cleared, and

(5) Latch circuit of the IBM 650 which consisted of combinational elements with feedback.

Binary memory elements may be classified into three broad categories. The first, the delay element, is a device with a single binary-valued input and a binary-valued output. This memory element was used in clocked systems; in conjunction with feedback, it provided storage for one bit of information. The second type of memory element, the ac-coupled flip-flop, used a pulse or triggering spike to change the state. The triggering mechanism was a pulse of carefully controlled width of a gating circuit that passed a change in voltage level through a capacitor. Flip-flops triggered by the latter means were called edge-sensitive or transition-sensitive. The third kind of flip-flop, the dc-coupled flip-flop, used level signals to change the state. This flip-flop operated independently of rise or fall times and did not require an input with a narrow pulse-width.

In summary, the first generation computer engineers pioneered many diverse logic circuits, coupling schemes and system timings. It was a period of great experimentation where many different logic design and hardware circuit techniques were attempted. Even in relay machines there were the two methods of control: the Harvard Mark II had a pulse distributor to provide synchronization, whereas the Bell Telephone Laboratory machines generally used a completion signal to activate the next step.

3. Early Controversies

As might be expected, some of the computer pioneers had definite opinions about their particular design approach. Aside from the architectural debates that existed (fixed word length versus variable word length, decimal versus binary, the best way to represent negative numbers, etc.), there were two loosely connected controversies related to logic design and sequential machine theory. The first dispute concerned the reliability of ac coupling versus dc coupling of circuits. The other debate concerned the fastest scheme for central processor system timing, the utilization of a clock to divide time into increments for controlling information flow versus the utilization of a completion signal related to the circuit speed to initiate the next operation. These questions are considered in the next two sections.

a. Coupling: ac or dc?

Another name used for direct coupled system was *level logic*. When the ac coupling was used with pulses (as opposed to level shifts), the term *pulse logic* was used. Gray [22] mentions that some of the advantages of pulse logic systems were "the possibility of the use of ac coupling devices such as capacitors and transformers and the possibility of obtaining more power and less delay in circuit-limited operation because of less-than-unity duty factor."† Richards [6] also mentions the good fan-out capability. The Computer Handbook [23] points out another advantage: with the use of pulse transformers and short-duration pulse transmission at low impedance, there is good matching to low impedance transmission lines. A disadvantage of dc coupling with vacuum tubes was the difference in dc levels required by the input terminal and those provided by the output terminal. A resistor divider not only attenuated the signal but also presented such a relatively high impedance that cathode followers were required before any significant load could be driven.

The use of pulse inputs to memory elements introduced some complex timing problems. Wood [24] studied the problem in considerable detail. In general, there are minimum and maximum specifications for the pulse width and a minimum specification on the recovery time. For pulse output systems, a problem existed in ensuring the inputs reached an AND gate at the proper time. To avoid resynchronization problems, many of the pulse input memory elements provided level outputs. One way to use these outputs was found in the Whirlwind I, where a level signal acted as a gate to a pulse. Another method that utilized these outputs was a differentiating network of Fig. 1.6 that provided a triggering pulse.

A complementing (or toggle) flip-flop (or binary trigger) is a flip-flop that always changes state upon being triggered. Complementing triggers with level outputs and edge-sensitive (i.e., triggering on either the negative-going edge or positive-going edge but not both) inputs could be cascaded to form a binary ripple carry counter. A problem with edge-sensitive circuits is that care must be taken to prevent noise spikes from generating unwanted results. Figure 1.11 shows an example of a counter for negative-edge sensitive input memory elements. (This type of counter circuit was used in counting outputs of Geiger tubes long before its use in computers.) In the particular circuit shown, the counter counts *modulo 8* in binary, that is, it counts from 0 through 7 in binary, then repeats. The flip-flop element changes state on the negative-going transition of its input. Assuming the counter begins at 000 (in binary), the first negative clock changes the counter to 001. The second clock pulse complements the first flip-flop (as always) but now the first flip-flop output experiences a negative-going transition, which complements the second flip-flop. The count is now 010. The count proceeds in this manner, advancing with each clock pulse, as shown in the timing chart of Fig. 1.11.

† From Harry J. Gray, "Digital Computer Engineering." © 1963, Prentice-Hall, Inc., Englewood Cliffs, New Jersey. Reprinted by permission of the publishers.

Proponents for dc coupling felt that ac coupling had some disadvantages, particularly in the area of reliability. Brooks and Iverson [16], mentioned dc coupling meant less sensitivity to variations of circuit components and signals. A discussion of ac versus dc coupling appears in Richards [6], where he mentions that the suspected unreliability is attributed to the fact that both the amplitude and the rise and/or fall times of a pulse must be within tolerances, when passed through a capacitor (as used in Fig. 1.6, for example.) The advocates of the ac coupled trigger disputed the reliability argument (ENIAC experience had shown little trouble with capacitors) and claimed the trigger, which responded to a change-of-level rather than a dc level, represented a much more powerful logic block; they also asserted that certain logic could be accomplished more simply and more economically with triggers than with latches. In practice, a mixed strategy between ac and dc coupling was often found [23] as in the IBM 650 or NAREC. In the IBM 702 diode gate system, only pulses from the clock (where rise and fall times were controlled) actuated the memory elements.

b. Fastest System Timing Scheme: Synchronous or Asynchronous?

The question of "clocked" versus self-timed philosophies has existed for a long time. In 1948 Stibitz stated, "there are in use at present two general plans of internal organization. In one plan, each component operation is

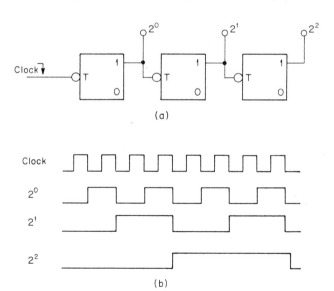

(a)

(b)

Fig. 1.11. Binary counter with ripple carry using edge-sensitive complementing flip-flops. (a) Schematic diagram. (b) Timing chart.

assigned a definite place in the time scale of the machine's operation. In a machine designed on this plan, each addition, each multiplication, and each reading of data takes place at a prescribed part of the time cycle. The alternative plan is that in which the completion of one operation signals the control mechanism to start the next operation" [25].†

The completion signal was the key to asynchronous timing. Earle [26] stated it was the "essential characteristic," whereas in synchronous operation the spacing (in time) of the clock signals was used to "wait out" the worst-case delay times of the circuits.

Richards noted that system timing was very different between the IAS computer and the SEAC [1]. He pointed out the "speed advantage" claim for asynchronous operation was much more complex than the fact asynchronous operations did not wait on timing signals from a clock. Wilkes, in comparing relay machines, sounded a note of caution [27]. He observed that asynchronous systems need not necessarily result in faster operation because more relay operations were needed than in a corresponding synchronous system. Brooks and Iverson [16] echoed similar thoughts. Where the times involved were relatively insensitive to the data, as in the addition of two digits, the IBM 650 used synchronous operation; whereas in the case of loading a register from drum storage, which could vary by a factor of 50, completion signalling was used. Another point considered by Richards [1] was the data rate limit on the storage unit. If the circuits in a clocked system were fast enough (assuming worst-case delay) to keep up with the memory unit, then any additional speed from asynchronous timing would not improve the performance.

Another factor is the method by which the completion signal is generated. There are several ways of obtaining a completion signal. In the IAS computer, a slower acting prototype toggle was used during shifting operations. Another method was use of the 12-microsecond delay for the adder. Neither of these methods improved performance over the synchronous scheme because in either case the time allotted for the operation had to exceed the worst-case time. Only when the completion signal denoted actual completion (such as in the NAREC where a comparator circuit compared source and destination register contents to ensure the data transfer had transpired) could an improvement in speed be made. However, the asynchronous system must suffer a delay to generate the completion signal, plus a delay in changing the control state of the computer to get the next operation started. Thus, where operations may take

† From G. R. Stibitz, The organization of large-scale calculating machinery, *Annals of the Harvard Computation Laboratory* **16**. © 1948, Harvard Univ. Press, Cambridge, Massachusetts. Reprinted by permission.

almost as much time as the worst-case delay, the time for generating the completion signal might cause the asynchronous scheme to be slower than the synchronous.

There is another point that should be discussed and that is cycle time. If the worst-case delay through an adder is 500 nanoseconds, it generally can be cycled at close to a 500-nanosecond rate in a synchronous environment. That is, the adder can be presented with new input values every 500 nanoseconds. Consider an asynchronously controlled adder presented with valid inputs. Upon receipt of the completion signal, the adder must next enter a "relaxation phase" where no valid input is presented to the adder and the completion signal circuitry becomes inactive. If after receiving a completion signal, the asynchronous system control immediately presented the adder with new valid inputs, then a premature completion signal might result. Thus, in the clocked situation the equipment can be recycled immediately, while in the asynchronous case the equipment cannot be immediately recycled.

In general, asynchronous operation could be faster where the worst-case delay was considerably longer than a typical delay or where a completion signal could be achieved at little cost. Today, clocked operation is prevalent within the central processor, and reply-back signals are most often used in the input/output areas of a system.

C. Discrete Transistor Technology

In 1948 the transistor was invented [28]; subsequent use of discrete transistor technology in computers characterized the *second generation* machines. On October 7, 1954, an all-transistor IBM 604 calculator was demonstrated publicly. Earlier that year, Bell Telephone Labs placed a 700 transistor computer, TRADIC (Transistor Digital Computer), on life test. In April 1956, Lincoln Laboratory of MIT completed the TX-0, a 3600 transistor computer. In 1955, the UNIVAC LARC (Livermore Atomic Research Computer), a large-scale transistor computer, was announced; and Philco built the TRANSAC (Transistor Automatic Computer) under government contract.

Most of the initial transistor logic circuits were, understandably enough, conversions of vacuum tube logic. Kudlich designed transistor circuits suitable for use in computers similar to the IAS computer [29]. A transistorized version of the "pulse former" used in the UNIVAC I was used in the UNIVAC LARC [22]. The vacuum tube gated pulse amplifiers and flip-flops of the Whirlwind I were transistorized for use in the TX-O and its successor the TX-2 [30]. A transistor circuit that could replace the SEAC

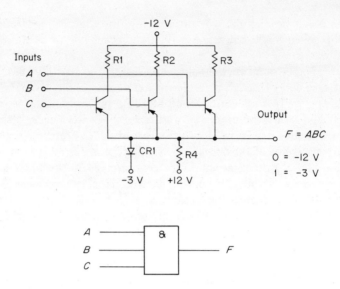

Fig. 1.12.   A three-input AND circuit in DCTL and its logic symbol.

pulse amplifier circuit was reported by Felker [31]. Wanlass [32] described a diode gate scheme where the clock signal appeared on the resistor of every diode AND. The AND gate outputs passed through a diode OR to set or reset a flip-flop. This scheme was logically reminiscent of the diode gate circuitry of the IBM 702 and IBM 705.

In 1954 Philco provided a breakthrough for high-speed computing when it developed the surface barrier transistor [33, 34]. Philco used this transistor for a logic family called direct-coupled transitor logic (DCTL) [34, 35]. A DCTL "AND" circuit is shown in Fig. 1.12. All inputs had to be at −3 V turning "off" the transistors, in order for the output to be at −3 V. With an input at −12 V, its transistor conducts, pulling point F down to −12 V since R1, R2, and R3 are small compared to R4. Flip-flop operation in this family was the "pull-over" type; this was like the IAS computer mode of operation. One of the disadvantages of DCTL was that it required one transistor for each input.

A popular technique, collectively called transistor–diode logic (TDL), used a diode OR or a diode AND which drove a transistor inverter and resulted in a NOR or NAND, respectively. This was derived from first generation schemes where diode AND or OR gates drive a vacuum tube inverter.

In late 1956 and early 1957 the transistor-resistor logic (TRL) gate was independently reported by two sources. [36–38]. This circuit, called a NOR by Rowe, is shown in Fig. 1.13. The capacitors across the input resistors were for "speed-up" purposes (see Fig. 1.13). The circuit was called a NOR because it performed an OR function followed by a NOT function. Rowe considered the active voltage (or 1-state) to be -20 V; the ground voltage was the 0-state. With respect to Fig. 1.13a, if any of the inputs are a 1 (-20 V), then base-emitter current flows and the transistor turns on, grounding the output. With all inputs at ground, no base-emitter current flows and the transistor behaves as an open circuit. The output approaches -20 V. Figure 1.13b behaves in a similar manner, except the "high" voltage is $+6$ V and the "low" voltage is clamped to ground by a diode. If the high voltage (ground) were viewed as the 1-state and the low voltage (-20 V) as the 0-state, then the circuit would perform the NAND function, instead of the NOR function.

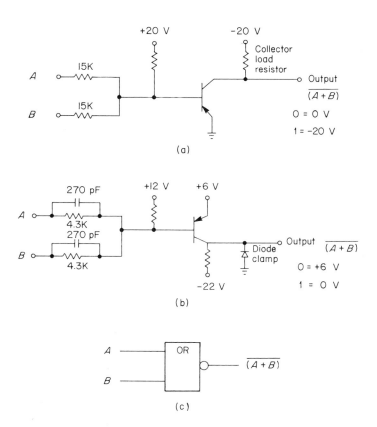

Fig. 1.13. The TRL NOR circuit. (a) Rowe version. (b) Cole *et al.* version. (c) Logic symbol.

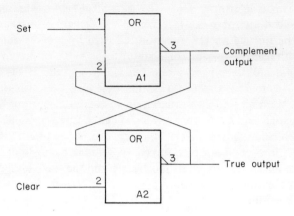

Fig. 1.14. NOR flip-flop.

Rowe [36] observed that the TRL circuit was not a mere replacement of vacuum tubes and diodes in computer circuits. Cole *et al.* [38] viewed the circuit as a means to avoid pulse techniques. The NOR circuit could be used to synthesize any Boolean function and could be cross-coupled to form a level-sensitive flip-flop (see Fig. 1.14). Assume the flip-flop stores a 0, and that it is neither being set or cleared. The inputs 2 of NORs A1 and A2 are in the 0-state. Output 3 of NOR A2 is in the 0-state to reflect the storage of a 0. With both inputs of NOR A1 in the 0-state, its output is in the 1-state. The flip-flop is stable because input 1 of NOR A2 "holds" output 3 of NOR A2 in the 0-state. To set the flip-flop (so it stores a "1"), input 1 of NOR A1 causes output 3 of NOR A1 to go to the 0-state. Both inputs of NOR A2 are now in the 0-state and its output goes to the 1-state. This 1-state is fed back to NOR A1, "holding" output 3 of NOR A1 to the 0-state even after the "set" input returns to the 0-state. This type of analysis is known as "chasing ones and zeroes" and can be used by the reader to analyze the way the flip-flop is cleared (reset to 0).

In a survey paper, Henle (see Henle and Walsh [39]) described the NOR as being economical where high-speed was not required. For its high performance STRETCH computer project, announced in 1956, IBM selected the current switch [40, 41]. These circuits were designed to have two complementary outputs: the in-phase and the out-of-phase. The circuits functioned as an OR–NOR or AND–NAND.

Development also proceeded on the design of ac-coupled bistable transistor memory elements. In Fig. 1.15 is shown a widely used resistance-gated diode trigger circuit, which is described by Henle [39]. The flip-flop is edge-sensitive; triggering took place on the negative edge. At the time (1958), Henle noted it was economical and found applications in rings, counters, and shifting registers.

Another edge-sensitive flip-flop circuit was used in the IBM 1401 [42]. This circuit made use of the diode gate described earlier in connection with the IBM 702. This type of transistor trigger or "pedestal trigger" [43] could function like most of the popular clocked memory elements by manipulating the inputs.

Packaging for these circuits generally took the form of discrete components mounted on a printed circuit card. Riggs [44] covers some of the packages that were commercially available in 1961. The IBM package, called SMS (Standard Modular System), was used in packaging of the IBM 1401 and IBM 7090 [45].

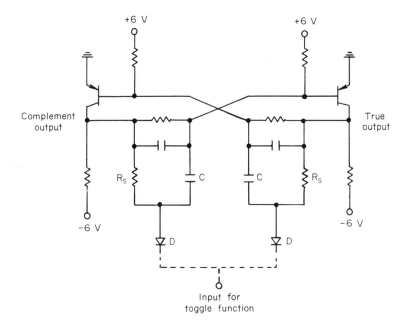

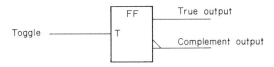

Fig. 1.15.   The resistance-gated diode trigger, a complementing flip-flop.

The second generation of computers decreased their use of a job completion signal timing within the central processor (the Illiac II and TRANSAC being notable exceptions). With the advent of magnetic core main memories, most machine designs were oriented to the timing of the main memory cycle, and clocked operations prevailed. A variety of clocking schemes was seen. For example, the basic timing cycle of the IBM 1401 was divided into eight time increments, but the basic clock used four triggers whose operations overlapped: each trigger was "on" for four increments and "off" for four increments. Individual timing signals that were needed could be generated by forming the appropriate AND function of the basic trigger clock signals.

With the advent of the transistor, some of the problems of the first generation disappeared, i.e., the mismatch between the input and output impedance and voltage levels, and the strong motivation for pulsed circuits. The logic circuit families consisted of dc-coupled decision elements (generally DCTL, TRL, DTL, or current-switch type from which combinational functions could be synthesized) and possibly some edge-sensitive memory elements. Where edge-sensitive memory elements were not used, the combinational gates themselves could be interconnected with feedback as in Fig. 1.14 to form dc coupled or level-sensitive memory elements much like the IBM 650 latch or the set reset (SR) flip-flop of the IAS computer.

Although the dc-coupling philosophy expounded by the IAS computer designers prevailed in the second generation, the use of the job initiation and job completion signals within the central processor declined. The author can recall only TRANSAC (and its derivatives) built by Philco as using this system timing philosophy. In the second generation, the transistor circuits were often fast relative to the memory cycle, hence the internal performance of many systems was limited by the width and cycle time of main memory and not by worst-case gate delays.

Many of the minimization objectives employed by logic designers in the first generation were also changed. For example, in designing combinational nets where the AND and OR functions could be performed by relatively inexpensive diode logic but inversion required a vacuum tube for inversion, a premium was placed on circuits that minimized the number of inverters. Also, in circuits with feedback (sequential circuits), amplification was required in each feedback loop, and therefore a circuit with fewer feedback loops tended to be less expensive. The second generation technology, which provided inversion and amplification with each gate, rendered both these minimization objectives obsolete.

D. Monolithic Integrated Circuit Technology

In the early 1960s the semiconductor industry turned toward the technology of the third generation, the monolithic integrated circuit (IC). The term monolithic (Greek for "single stone") refers to the single piece of silicon in which the circuits are made. The planar silicon transistor technology which could produce transistors and diodes of small size and low cost could also make the interconnection between components. The components and interconnections are fabricated in successive steps on a single substrate to produce an integrated circuit. Transistors and diodes are formed from semiconductor junctions. Resistors, less precisely produced, are made by controlling the length, width, and depth of semiconductor diffusion. Capacitors also are available in integrated circuit technology, but they take up a lot of area. A brief history on bipolar combinational gates appears in the book by Wickes [46].

1. Bipolar Combinational Gates

In 1961 Fairchild marketed a logic family under the name Micrologic. It was basically a DCTL circuit (see Fig. 1.12) with resistors added to the bases to prevent "current hogging," and the basic circuit type was called RTL (resistor–transistor logic; see Fig. 1.16).

In 1961 Texas Instruments introduced a family called Series SN51. The

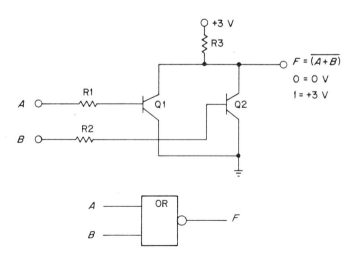

Fig. 1.16. Fairchild micrologic RTL circuit.

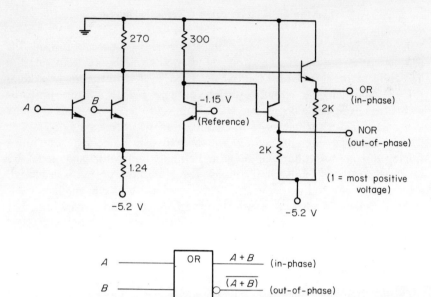

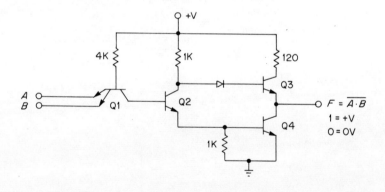

Fig. 1.17. Motorola emitter-coupled logic.

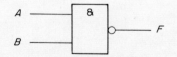

Fig. 1.18. The TTL (or T²L) circuit of the Sylvania SUHL I line.

basic circuit looked like the RTL circuit of Fig. 1.6, but the capacitors were placed across resistors R1 and R2 to speed up switching at the expense of a little more power. A DTL (diode–transistor logic) line of monolithic integrated circuits was subsequently introduced by Signetics. Also in 1961, General Electric introduced the current switch in a family of integrated circuits called ECLO (emitter-coupled logic operators). Motorola also introduced this type of integrated circuit an called it MECL (Motorola emitter-coupled logic; see Fig. 1.17). This circuit was interesting because both true (in-phase) and complement (out-of-phase) output polarities were available. This circuit was also called current switch emitter follower (CSEF) or current mode logic (CML).

A new kind of circuit, called transistor–transistor logic was reported by Beeson and Ruegg [47]. In 1963, Sylvania was one of the first manufacturers to introduce transistor–transistor logic (T^2L or TTL). This circuit, very similar to DTL, had the diode AND at the input of the transistor replaced by a single multiple-emitter transistor. With an active transistor replacing the input diodes, much higher switching speeds were achieved. The family line, called SUHL I (Sylvania Universal High-Level Logic), is shown in Fig. 1.18. Transistors Q3 and Q4 are in the push-pull output, pull-up network which provides rapid charging or discharging of a capacitive load and good noise immunity. Unfortunately the totem pole (as it is called) makes the "DOT-OR" or "WIRE-OR" function more difficult to implement.

Wickes [46] stated that the four basic forms of the combinational integrated circuit gates are DCTL, DTL, T^2L, and CML. Most other available integrated circuits are variations of these basic types. Lo [48] stated that the TRL and DCTL have been obsoleted in favor of DTL and T^2L for cost-oriented applications and CML for performance-oriented applications. The TTL technology, using a 5-V ($\pm10\%$) supply, is currently the predominant bipolar transistor technology.

2. Bipolar Memory Elements

The IC bipolar memory elements are generally one of four varieties. One variety, the cross-coupled NOR flip-flops, latches, or polarity-hold (also called D-type latch, data hold, or sample and hold) memory elements are built from the combinational gates, have a single feedback loop, and are not edge-sensitive. The remaining three memory element types (capacitor charge, master–slave, and D-type) are considered to be edge-sensitive. Due to the difficulty and expense of making integrated circuit capacitors, ac-coupled memory elements are not popular, and pulse-type circuits are absent.

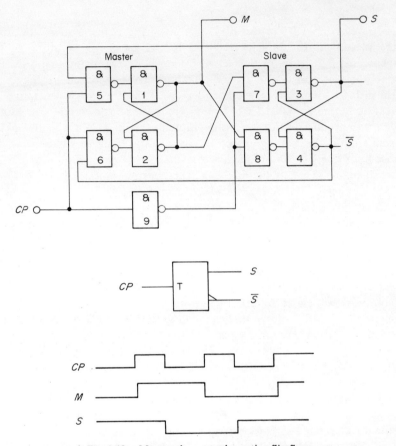

Fig. 1.19. Master–slave complementing flip-flop.

Camenzind of Signetics [49] describes a "center point triggered charge control" flip-flop where two transistors stored a measured amount of charge for a short time in the base-collector diode. Upon triggering by a negative-going edge, the amount of charge was large enough such that when released to the base of another transistor, it was sufficient to cause switching. Davies and Hamlin of Fairchild describe the detail the operation of an edge-sensitive *JK* flip-flop which also uses the charge in the collector-base junction of a transistor [50]. A similar *JK* flip-flop appears in a survey article by the editors of EDN [51]. An integrated circuit *JK* edge-sensitive flip-flop which used capacitors was described by Landers and Garth [52] of Motorola.

To avoid the need for capacitors, designers turned from the ac coupling of edge-sensitive flip-flops to the use of constructing the same function from dc-coupled decision elements. A *master–slave,* complementing flip-flop (Fig. 1.19) is described by Camenzind [49]. This flip-flop was related to the double rank counter stage used in the IAS computer. This binary counter element contains a *critical race* during the 0–1 transition of the clock signal. A critical race exists when signals along two or more paths are changing simultaneously and where there is a path which, if it changes before others, will cause a malfunction. A malfunction can occur when S is in the 0-state and gate 9 is slower than gates 6 and 2 combined. (When S is in the 1-state, the race is between gate 9 and gates 5 and 1.) The race can be eliminated by eliminating the offending gate, gate 9. This is done by fanning out gate 5 to gates 7 and 8, and also by fanning out gate 6 to gates 7 and 8. The race is no longer between gates, and it is virtually eliminated since it is between an interconnection delay and a gate delay (including the interconnection delays to and from that gate). When a race is no longer between gates, the circuit has been termed "reliable" by Maley and Earle [53].

The complementing master–slave flip-flop can be modified to behave as a clocked (or three-input) JK flip-flop under certain conditions. A variation of the circuit (Fig. 1.20) which operates reliably appears in Sepe [54]. Change of state occurs when the C input makes the 1–0 transition. The JK flip-flop is a marriage of the set–reset flip-flop and the complementing flip-

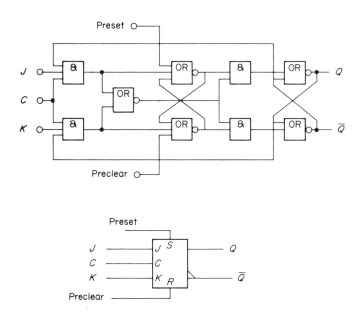

Fig. 1.20. A clocked (three-input) JK master–slave flip-flop.

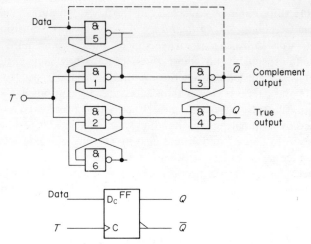

Fig. 1.21. *D*-Type edge-sensitive flip-flop.

flop with the *J* input serving to set the flip-flop and the *K* input serving to reset it. If inputs *J* and *K* are both 0 when *C* is in the 1-state, then the flip-flop output remains unchanged. If inputs *J* and *K* are both 1 when *C* is in the 1-state, then the *JK* flip-flop behaves as a complementing flip-flop. This flip-flop differs from the so-called "asynchronous" or two-input *JK* flip-flop mentioned in connection with the ENIAC. However, care must be taken to ensure that inputs *J* and *K* do not change state while input *C* is in the 1-state; otherwise the flip-flop could erroneously change state. In this sense, the master–slave flip-flop more closely resembles the pulse-sensitive flip-flops because many designers use a narrow pulse width for the signal at input *C*. The PRESET and PRECLEAR inputs are so-called because to set or clear the flip-flop properly, the *C* input must be in the 0-state.

Another memory element is the *D-type edge-sensitive* flip-flop (see Fig. 1.21). This circuit advanced the state-of-the-art and was, to this writer's knowledge, first discovered and reported by Earle [26]. The edge-sensitive *D*-type flip-flop is similar to a polarity-hold (PH) flip-flop except that the *D*-type flip-flop changes to the state of its *D* input only on the 0–1 transition of its control (*C*) input. It is very useful for constructing data registers, counters, or shift registers. It only has two inputs instead of the three found in the clocked *JK* flip-flop and hence involves fewer "pins" to wire. The reader should be warned of the ambiguity of the term "D-flip-flop" which may mean either the *D*-type or the PH. By connecting the complement output to the *D* input (dotted line, Fig. 1.21), a complementing flip-flop (toggle) may be constructed. This circuit has a critical race; however, it is between an interconnection delay and a gate delay with its associated interconnection delays and thus operates reliably. The detailed operation of this circuit is described in Maley and Earle [53], and the gate numbers correspond to their figure. Another version of this circuit appears in Boag [55], who describes the Siliconix A03 chip, and demonstrates that by properly manipulating the signals, the circuit can perform *JK*, set–reset, or complementing functions.

3. Second and Third Generation Timing Schemes

The logic and timing schemes of the second and third generations generally either could be likened to that of the IBM 650, where level-sensitive flip-flops are used for data storage, or the IBM 702 which used edge-sensitive flip-flops. The timing cycle was usually divided into four or eight timing "points" or "clock-times." First consider level-sensitive flip-flops that are changed during a particular clock time, say clock A. We require that the inputs to the combinational circuit (see Fig. 1.7) supplying the set, reset, or data flip-flop inputs be stable during clock A. Hence the flip-flop outputs that influence the set of flip-flops changed during clock A must themselves be changed at some other clock-time. For machines that use edge-sensitive flip-flops, this timing restriction does not exist and flip-flops changed at clock A can feed other flip-flops changed at clock A. However, edge-sensitive flip-flops are more complex (hence more costly) than level-sensitive flip-flops, so in many designs both types are found. Level-sensitive flip-flops are employed where the timing restriction is not bothersome, and edge-sensitive flip-flops are employed in circuits like counters, shift registers, and in certain accumulator registers. The selection of which clock pulse in the cycle is to clock a particular flip-flop depends on when the flip-flops feeding the combinational circuit become ready, and on the "worst-case" delay through that combinational circuit. This topic is covered in Chapter 3 under "System Timing."

4. Hybrid Circuits

The superiority of integrated circuits in the middle 1960s was not universally accepted; for example, in 1964 IBM introduced a hybrid circuit technology called SLT (Solid Logic Technology) for the System/360 computer family [56]. In SLT, the transistors and diodes are interconnected to form the logic circuit by a printed circuit on the chip carrier, a half-inch-square white ceramic. IBM felt at the time that this was the most economical approach [57]. It has since introduced MST (Monolithic Systems

Technology) which uses a monolithic current-switch, emitter–follower circuit. Another exception to the use of monolithic integrated circuits is the CDC 7600 computer announced by Control Data Corporation in 1968, which uses very densely packaged discrete components. CDC stated at the time of announcement that integrated circuits were not as fast or reliable as discrete components for this application [58].

5. FET Technology

The preceding discussion was confined to bipolar (p-n junction) transistors. This transistor is called bipolar because it depends on the flow of both majority and minority carriers. In 1968, Bloch and Henle [59] noted that bipolar transistor technology dominated data processing systems, with only MOS FET (metal–oxide–semiconductor field-effect transistors) as a possible challenger. The field-effect transistor (FET) first described by W. Shockley in 1952, more closely resembles a vacuum tube triode than any other semiconductor device. The FET source electrode, gate electrode, and drain electrode are analogous to the cathode, grid, and anode, respectively, of the triode. Field-effect transistors are employed as the basic switching element of the AND and OR gates. The FET is a unipolar device and the flow of majority carriers in the channel between the source and drain electrodes is controlled by the electric charge on the gate electrode. The device is implemented in the metal–oxide–semiconductor (MOS) technology and requires a single diffusion for its fabrication. The earlier problems with cleanliness and achieving good process control have been solved and MOS FETs are now popular logic devices.

There are two general types of MOS FET circuits from the standpoint of logic design. The first is the conventional dc-coupled combinational logic gate. Placing MOS inverters in parallel provides a NOR gate, while connecting them in series gives a NAND function. Figure 1.22 shows two series inverters placed in parallel with a single inverter using a common load to provide an AND-OR-INVERT function. These circuits are called ratio-type static circuits [60]. The term *ratio* is used because the actual "down-level" (logical 0) of a circuit like Fig. 1.22 is influenced mainly by a "voltage divider" effect and depends upon the relative size or "ratio" of the load device as compared with the "drive" or gate devices. A technology for which this ratio problem does not exist as such, yet which provides static circuits, is C-MOS (for complementary MOS). At the expense of more process steps, and more devices for a given combinational gate, the C-MOS technology offers relatively good speed, high fan-out, excellent noise immunity, and very low power consumption. Static circuits behave like bipolar decision elements, hence the logic and timing schemes used with these MOS circuits are the same as those found in bipolar technologies. The edge-sensitive D and the JK master–slave flip-flops can just as easily be constructed from static MOS logic gates.

In Fig. 1.22, we view voltage levels within a few volts of $+V$ to be 1 and within a few volts of ground to be 0. (In many applications, the voltage source is between 8 and 15 V.) If input C is in the 1-state, then that gate device is on (conducts), and output F becomes 0, because most of the source voltage appears across the load device. If input C is in the 0-state, that device is off; but if inputs A and B are both in the 1-state, then another conducting path to ground is provided, and output F becomes 0. When gate device C is off, and either A or B is off, then no conducting path exists, and output F approaches to within its "threshold voltage" (about 2 V) of voltage level V. This is sufficient to give an output of 1. The logical function of the circuit is also shown in block diagram form.

The second form is the dynamic (ratioless) logic circuit. These are popular because they achieve a large reduction in power and chip area per function relative to static circuits. The gate capacitance of the MOS device

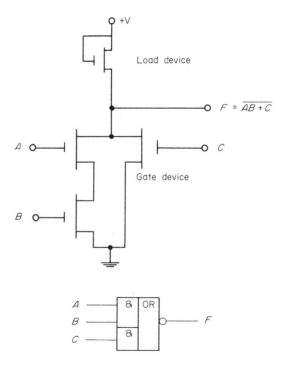

Fig. 1.22. N-Channel MOS AND–OR–INVERT function.

is used to store a charge temporarily. Multiphase clocking, generally four phase, provides direction to the flow of information. The charge, due to parasitic leakage currents, will not remain indefinitely. That is why FET shift registers, made in dynamic logic, must be shifted at some minimum rate (e.g., 10 kHz) or the information is lost. Dynamic MOS logic is reminiscent of magnetic logic [61], and of a transistor pulsed circuit scheme described in 1955 by Wanless [32], where the clock signal provides both the power and synchronization. From an abstract system timing viewpoint, these circuits have much in common with the SEAC model, although the four SEAC phases do not correspond to the four phases of dynamic MOS.

Since MOS technology includes fewer process steps than the bipolar technology, its advantages include higher yield, higher densities, lower power requirement, and higher reliability due to a simpler device. Disadvantages include slower speed and a need for interface circuits to communicate with the "outside" world.

Reliable MOS FET circuits have been developed more recently than bipolar circuits, and past experience would indicate they have a bright future as the "learning factors" bring further improvements. For further reading, a reference text on the general subject, which includes logic design and system design with MOS, is suggested [62].

6. Large-Scale Integration

Large-scale integration (LSI) is an evolutionary step for integrated circuit technology and generally implies a circuit density of hundreds or thousands of interconnected gates on a chip of 150–225 mils on a side. Such densities have been achieved in memories and in one-chip calculators, and multichip microcomputers. The term medium-scale integration (MSI) generally means a density of 40–100 gates per chip. LSI is here today, and prior to its arrival, much discussion had taken place on the utlilization of LSI in logic design. Opinions ranged from welcoming LSI as a means for providing computers with increased hardware functions for reducing software complexity, to the statement by Pollard [63] that the use of LSI can be considered only in areas where there is a high degree of repetition and a simplicity in the logic structure. The reason for not applying it in other areas is that in LSI one cannot readily correct logic bugs or modify the logic.

A trend characteristic of the computer industry has been the reduction in the cost of the hardware accompanied by an increase in the cost of the software (operating system or control program, compilers, assemblers, etc.) and applications programs. Many computer professionals may tend to view LSI as heralding "almost free" hardware and hence call for increased function from the hardware. This will happen, of course, but LSI is not "free," and brings with it new problems such that it must be employed rather carefully in computer systems. LSI has been successful in the very small computer (microcomputer or calculator) function and in memories, and is turning logic designers into microprocessor programmers. On the other hand, it is unclear to many how it should be applied in the logic of large systems.

In discussing the future of integrated circuits, Henle and Hill [64] specify problems facing the application of LSI. One, called the *engineering change* problem, results from the difficulty of making modifications in the field or during development which generally cause interconnections of the logic gates to be added and deleted. (The analogy with "patching" computer programs by adding and deleting instructions is very close.) Henle and Hill point out four reasons for these modifications:

(1) to add features,
(2) to improve performance,
(3) to correct bugs or improve timing margins, and
(4) to improve reliability and make the machine more easily serviced.

Another problem facing the application of LSI, called the "part number problem," is described, for example, by Farina *et al.* [65]. They felt that the chief obstacle facing the application of LSI was the "part number generation problem." If nonrepetitive functions are implemented in LSI, then the number of part numbers at the chip level increases. The fixed cost to generate the custom chip, including the changes made to it during debugging, might be too large to offer any overall cost savings.

One impact that the advent of smaller devices has had on computer logic is that now packaging has become an important consideration. Bloch and Henle [59] feel this to be the key problem area in electronics. In second generation systems, how the system was partitioned into printed circuit cards and where they were placed was not too critical because the circuits were less dense and could be interconnected by wire or cable in a convenient manner. Further, the relative cost of the interconnection system was low compared to the logic circuit cost. To get a better idea of the packaging problem, consider packaging techniques. Integrated circuits are made on a wafer which is then diced to form chips. Next the chips are bonded to the chip carrier package, the form in which the circuit is sold; this is called the first-level package. The second-level package is a printed circuit card or board which may be laminated with two or more layers of interconnections. The third level consists of plugging the card into a frame or large board which contains the "back panel" wiring or multilayer interconnections. Increased circuit speeds and nanosecond signal rise and fall times make the wires behave like transmission lines, with attendant reflections, and "ringing" problems if the *net* (points connected together) is too spread out or improperly terminated. Wiring complexity can be minimized by judicious partitioning into second-level packages, and by proper placement at both the second and third levels. This is even more true in LSI, and the designer tries to maximize the logic on a chip for the given number of signal pins or pads available. While device sizes have been shrinking dramatically (orders of magnitude) over the years, the size of contact pins and wire connections at the level where interconnections may be added or deleted have not kept pace. For example, integrated circuit package leads have had center-to-center spacings of 250 mils in the early 1960s, and have as small as a 50-mil spacing at present. This situation was foreseen in 1964 by Earle [66].

> In fact, we can envision the situation where a transistor that costs 3 cents will have a soldered connection that costs 10 cents. Generally the significant costs today—on or off the chip—are not the transistors but their interconnections and packages. To assess properly what should be minimized today, the logic designer must look to the packaging system, not to the components.†

So far, we have dealt with the "mainstream" of the technologies used in machine logic. Notable among the near successes are cryogenics, negative resistance devices (tunnel diodes), and magnetic core logic. Generally, most of these technologies have a counterpart in first generation technologies to which the logic designer can relate, for example, the cryotron behaves like the electromechanical relay. Magnetic logic including the parametron [67] can be related to multiphased pulsed logic. In fact the clocked dc-coupled logic and occasional use of edge-sensitive memory elements (prevalent in discrete and integrated circuit bipolar transistor technologies) is familiar to the logic designers of the IBM 650 computer. Thus, we can appreciate the comment of Richards [1] where he points out that although integrated circuits have reduced overall size and cost, they have not provided any new functions that could not have been performed with transistors or with the vacuum tube technology.

E. Review of Technology Developments

In the first generation many diverse schemes were tried, including dc coupling, ac coupling, completion signalling, and strictly clocked schemes.

† From John Earle, Digital computers—The impact of microelectronics, *Electronic Design*, December 7, 1964. © 1964, Hayden Publishing Company, Rochelle Park, New Jersey. Reprinted by permission.

With the advent of the transistor, and the ability of output signal levels to be used directly as input signal levels, a strong motivation for ac coupling disappeared. In the second generation, systems generally employed dc coupled level signals, with ac coupled triggers being used where convenient. The transistor gate possessed its own amplification; therefore the following requirement of many first generation machines disappeared: signal reamplification following a certain number of levels of diode AND–OR logic. Also, the problem of avoiding feedback with no amplification elements in the feedback loop disappeared. Instead of minimizing the diode count, logic designers worried about minimizing gates.

As the technology progressed to the bipolar integrated circuit, the difficulty and expense entailed by the capacitor further reduced the desirability of ac coupling and hence pulsed techniques. Schemes for achieving pulse-type operation with the edge-sensitive trigger function were employed, and then a dc coupled circuit of decision elements was devised to perform the edge-sensitive flip-flop function. Instead of minimizing gates, logic designers learned to minimize chips or interconnections. The notions of pulse-sensitive, edge-sensitive, and level-sensitive flip-flops have been presented. These notions are given more precise meaning in Chapter 3.

The approach of LSI has brought a resurgence of the pulse circuit system in the form of dynamic MOS FET technology. LSI has also focused on the packaging cost. Packaging has always had a strong interaction in the logic design of large, high-speed computer systems [68], but with LSI this strong influence is now extended down to most every digital system. The logic designer, to apply LSI successfully, is faced with the awesome tasks of simultaneously minimizing intermodule interconnections and part-numbers, and eliminating engineering change activity at the LSI chip level. A stronger dependence exists on digital system simulation and testing procedures. The testing problem may possibly bring about simpler system timing configurations, such as that used in the IBM S/360 Model 50 (see Chapter 3). It is relatively difficult to test an edge-sensitive flip-flop buried deep within an LSI chip.

A study of the logic and timing environment shows that there have appeared no new timing configurations or timing schemes which cannot be compared to a scheme found in some first generation machine. (A possible exception is the use of overlapped level clock signals.) This has been observed in a similar sense by Richards when he noted that one can perform with vacuum tubes any function that can be performed with transistors.

References

1. R. K. Richards, "Electronic Digital Systems." Wiley, New York, 1966.
2. M. H. Mickle, A compiler level program for teaching digital systems design. *IEEE Trans. Educ.* **E-12**, 274–279 (1969).
3. A. W. Burks, Electronic computing circuits of the ENIAC. *Proc. IRE* **35**, 756–767 (1947).
4. W. H. Eccles and F. W. Jordan, A trigger relay utilizing three-electrode thermionic vacuum tubes, *Radio Rev.* **1**, 143–146 (1919).
5. S. B. Williams, "Digital Computing Systems." McGraw-Hill, New York, 1959.
6. R. K. Richards, "Digital Computer Components and Circuits." Van Nostrand-Reinhold, Princeton, New Jersey, 1957.
7. A. L. Leiner, W. A. Notz, J. L. Smith, and A. Weinberger, System design of the SEAC and DYSEAC. *IRE Trans. Electron. Comput.* **EC-3** (2), 8–23 (1954).
8. R. D. Elbourn and R. P. Witt, Dynamic circuit techniques used in SEAC and DYSEAC. *IRE Trans. Electron. Comput.* **EC-2** (1), 2–9 (1953).
9. G. H. Mealy, A method for synthesizing sequential circuits. *Bell Syst. Tech. J.* **34**, 1045–1079 (1955).
10. C. E. Frizzell, Engineering description of the IBM type 701 computer. *Proc. IRE* **41**, 1275–1287 (1953).
11. W. J. Eckert and R. Jones, "Faster, Faster." McGraw-Hill, New York, 1955.
12. C. V. L. Smith, Electronic digital computers. *Advan. Electron.* **4**, 157–185 (1952).
13. R. R. Everett, The Whirlwind I computer. *Rev. Electron. Digital Comput. Joint AIEE-IRE Comput. Conf. Philadelphia, Pennsylvania, December 10–12, 1951*, pp. 70–74; published as *AIEE Special Publ.* **S-44** (1952).
14. M. M. Astrahan, B. Housman, J. F. Jacobs, R. P. Mayer, and W. H. Thomas, Logical design of the digital computer for the SAGE system. *IBM J. Res. Develop.* **1** (1), 76–83 (1957).
15. E. S. Hughes, Jr., Latch unit, U.S. Patent 2,628,309, February 10, 1953.
16. F. P. Brooks and K. E. Iverson, "Automatic Data Processing." Wiley, New York, 1963.
17. P. Sheretz, Electronic circuits of the NAREC computer. *Proc. IRE* **41**, 1313–1320 (1953).
18. G. Estrin, The electronic computer at the Institute for Advanced Study. *Math. Tables and Other Aids to Computation* **7**, 108–114 (1953).
19. R. E. Meagher and J. P. Nash, The ORDVAC. *Rev. Electron. Digital Comput. Joint AIEE-IRE Comput. Conf., Philadelphia, Pennsylvania, December 10–12, 1951*, pp. 37–43, published as *AIEE Special Publ.* **S-44** (1952).
20. W. H. Ware, The logical principles of a new kind of binary counter. *Proc. IRE* **41**, 1429–1447 (1953).
21. R. M. Brown, Some notes on logical binary counters. *IRE Trans. Electron. Comput.* **EC-4**, 67–69 (1955).
22. H. J. Gray, "Digital Computer Engineering." Prentice-Hall, Englewood Cliffs, New Jersey, 1963.
23. H. Huskey and G. Korn, eds., "Computer Handbook." McGraw-Hill, New York, 1962.
24. P. E. Wood, Jr., Hazards in pulse sequential circuits. *IEEE Trans. Electron. Comput.* **EC-13**, 151–153 (1964).
25. G. R. Stibitz, The organization of large-scale calculating machinery. *Ann. Harvard Comput. Lab. Proc. Symp. Large Scale Digital Comput. Mach., Cambridge, Massachusetts, January 1947*, **16**, pp. 91–100. Harvard Univ. Press, Cambridge, Massachusetts, 1948.

26. J. Earle, Logic and timing in digital system design. *Electron. Design* **8** (17), 30–42 (1961).
27. M. V. Wilkes, "Automatic Digital Computers." Wiley, New York, 1956.
28. J. Bardeen and W. H. Brattain, The transistor, a semiconductor triode. *Phys. Rev.* **74**, 230–231 (1948).
29. R. A. Kudlich, A set of transistor circuits for asynchronous direct-coupled computers. *Proc. AFIPS, Western Joint Comput. Conf., Los Angeles, California, March 1955*, **7**. AFIPS Press, Montvale, New Jersey, 1955.
30. K. H. Olsen, Transistor circuitry in the Lincoln TX-2. *Proc. AFIPS Western Joint Comput. Conf., Los Angeles, California, February 26–28, 1957*, pp. 167–170.
31. J. H. Felker, The transistor as a digital computer component. *Rev. Electron. Digital Comput. Joint AIEE-IRE Comput. Conf. Philadelphia, Pennsylvania, December 10–12, 1951*, published as *AIEE Special Publ.* **S-44**, pp. 105–109 (1952).
32. C. L. Wanlass, Transistor circuitry for digital computers. *IRE Trans. Electron. Comput.* **EC-4**, 11–15 (1955).
33. S. Rosen, Electronic computers: A historical survey. *Comput. Surveys* **1**, 7–36 (1969).
34. R. H. Beter, W. E. Bradley, R. B. Brown, and M. Rubinoff, Surface-barrier transistor switching circuits. *IRE Nat. Conv. Rec.* **3**, Pt. 4, 139–145 (1955).
35. R. H. Beter, W. E. Bradley, R. B. Brown, and M. Rubinoff, Directly coupled transistor circuits. *Electronics* **28** (6), 132–136 (1955).
36. W. D. Rowe, The transistor NOR circuit. *IRE WESCON Conv. Rec.* **1**, Pt. 4, 231–245 (1957).
37. W. D. Rowe and G. H. Royer, Transistor NOR circuit design. *Trans. AIEE* **76**, Pt. 1, 263–267 (1957).
38. C. T. Cole, Jr., K. L. Chien, and C. H. Prosper, Jr., A transistorized transcribing card punch. *Proc. AFIPS Eastern Joint Comput. Conf., December 10–12, 1956*, **10**, *AIEE Publ.* **T-92**, pp. 80–83.
39. R. A. Henle and J. L. Walsh, The Application of transistors to computers. *Proc. IRE* **46**, 1240–1254 (1968).
40. J. L. Walsh, IBM current mode transistor logical circuits, *Proc. AFIPS Western Joint Comput. Conf., Los Angeles, California, May 6–8, 1958*, **13**, pp. 34–36.
41. Transistor theory and application, IBM Form 223-6783. IBM, 1958, 1959. (Available from IBM Branch offices.)
42. Transistor component circuits. IBM Form S223-6889. IBM 1959, 1960, 1961. (Available from IBM Branch Offices.)
43. W. H. Libaw, Flip-flop comparisons for clocked digital systems. *Electron. Design News* **10** (8), 28–35 (1965).
44. J. R. Riggs, Digital logic modules. *Electro-Technol.* (*N.Y.*) **73**, 9 (1961).
45. Standard modular system. IBM Form S223-6900. IBM, 1959, 1960, 1961, 1962.
46. W. E. Wickes, "Logic Design with Integrated Circuits." IBM, Wiley, New York, 1968.
47. R. H. Beeson and H. W. Ruegg, New forms of all-transistor logic. *IEEE Int. Solid-State Circuits Conf., Philadelphia, Pennsylvania, 1962*, Digest, pp. 10–11, 104.
48. A. W. Lo, High-speed logic and memory—Past, present, and future. *Proc. AFIPS Fall Joint Comput. Conf., San Francisco, California, 1968*, **33**, pp. 1459–1465. Thompson, Washington, D.C., 1968.
49. H. R. Camenzind, Digital integrated circuit design techniques. *Comput. Design* **7** (11), 52–62 (1968).
50. D. C. Davies and W. O. Hamlin, J-K flip-flop reduces circuit complexity. *Electron. Design* **12** (6), 62–64 (1964).
51. Anon., eds., Digital complexity in 1968. *Electron. Design News* **13** (3), 30–40 (1968).

52. G. Landers and E. Garth, Simple technique speeds J-K counter design. *Electron. Design* **13** (15), 52–59 (1965).

53. G. A. Maley and J. Earle, "The Logical Design of Transistor Digital Computers." Prentice-Hall, Englewood Cliffs, New Jersey, 1963.

54. R. Sepe, How to synchronize pulses with only two flip-flops. *Electron. Eng.* **40** (6), 58–60 (1968).

55. T. R. Boag, Practical applications of an IC counter/shift register. *Electron. Design News* **10** (6), 18–27 (1965).

56. E. M. Davis, W. Harding, R. Schwartz, and J. Corning, Solid logic technology: Versatile, high-performance microelectronics. *IBM J. Res. Develop.* **8** (2), 102–114 (1964).

57. Close-up on tiny world of circuits. *IBM Magazine* **1**, 9 (1969).

58. *EDP Ind. Rep.* **4** (8), 2 (1968).

59. E. Bloch and R. A. Henle, Advances in circuit technology and their impact on computing systems. *In* "Information Processing 68" (A. J. H. Morrell, ed.), pp. 613–629. North-Holland Publ., Amsterdam, 1969.

60. R. F. Spencer, Jr., MOS complex gates in digital systems design. *IEEE Comput. Group News* **2** (11), 47–56 (1969).

61. A. J. Meyerhoff, G. Barnes, S. Disson, and G. Lund, "Digital Applications of Magnetic Devices." Wiley, New York, 1960.

62. W. M. Penney and L. Lau, "MOS Integrated Circuits." Van Nostrand-Reinhold, Princeton, New Jersey, 1972.

63. B. Pollard, G. Hollander, J. P. Eckert, Jr., and M. Palevsky, Impact of LSI on the next generation of computers (condensed panel discussion at the *IEEE Comput. Group Conf., 1968*). *Comput. Design* **8** (6), 48–59 (1969).

64. R. A. Henle and L. O. Hill, Integrated computer circuits—Past, present and future. *Proc. IEEE* **54**, 1849–1860 (1966).

65. D. E. Farina, G. C. Feth, H. L. Parks, and M. G. Smith, Large-scale integration perspectives. *IEEE Comput. Group News* **2** (6), 24–32 (1968).

66. J. Earle, Digital computers—The impact of microelectronics. *Electron. Design* **12**, 23 (1964) (also appeared as IBM TR 00.1236) (1965).

67. E. Goto, The parametron, a digital computing element which utilizes parametric oscillation. *Proc. IRE* **47**, 1304–1316 (1959).

68. M. J. Flynn and G. M. Amdahl, Engineering aspects of large high-speed computer design. *Symp. Microelectron. Large Systems, Washington, D.C., 1964*, pp. 77–95. Spartan Books, Washington, D.C., 1964.

Chapter 2

Theoretical Models and Synthesis Procedures

Chapter 1 describes many technologies used by engineers in designing computers. The use of these technologies in various logic and timing configurations produced several interesting models. These models, achieved by making simplifying assumptions, were used by investigators to study analysis and synthesis procedures for sequential machine theory. This chapter describes these models and their basic assumptions; where possible, the technology or computer that inspired the *model* will be noted.

S. Seshu [1] has defined a mathematical model as "the device by which we try to understand some aspect of the world about us, be it natural or man-made." He noted that at present, "empirical methods and experience are more useful tools than formal design techniques," but that "the intuition that we gain from a study of a mathematical model is extremely valuable; even if we completely disregard the formal design procedures."† He also pointed out that it is just as useless to view a large-scale computer as one sequential machine as it is to write the loop and node equations for a hi-fi audio amplifier. The approach has always been to break up the analysis into stages depending on the complexity of the system, as Moore [2] observed. Phister [3] also made this same point, calling it the "divide and conquer" approach. In the models that follow, it is tacitly assumed that the sequential circuit studied is embedded in an *environment* which supplies it with inputs and accepts its outputs. For this discussion, a *be-*

---

† From Sundarem Seshu, Mathematical Models for Sequential Machines. *IRE National Convention Record* 7 (2), pp. 4–16, © 1959. Reprinted by permission of the IEEE.

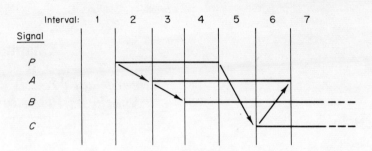

Fig. 2.1. A sequence diagram.

havioral description of a circuit is considered primarily to be a description of the circuit response to its inputs or input changes; a *structural description* is a logic diagram or set of Boolean equations which shows how the decision elements (gates) and memory elements (flip-flops) are interconnected.

In addition to the models, the following topics are covered in this section: analysis and synthesis tools, simplifying assumptions regarding sequential circuit input changes, stray delays in the circuits, and malfunctions. Also studied are equivalent transformations between two different abstract models. Attempts to classify the models and provide unified approaches to sequential machine theory are also reviewed. Combinational switching theory, which includes Boolean algebra, is not reviewed; the reader is assumed to have at least a slight familiarity with this subject.

A. Early Methods of Relay Design

Before presenting the more formal models that have evolved for sequential switching circuits, it is interesting to describe the prior state-of-the art. An excellent reference for this purpose is a book by Keister *et al.* [4] published in 1951. It seems appropriate that this book, the first in the field, was written at Bell Telephone Laboratories since switching theory was developed by the telephone industry and was strongly motivated by the intricacies of the dial telephone system. Many of the general principles found in the book are valid today. The following section, dealing with early relay technology, uses this book as a primary reference.

1. Timing Charts

Most of the early switching circuit techniques were developed for dial telephone centrals, where the relay was the basic component. The behavior of sequential switching circuits was described by time charts, sequence diagrams, or tabular sequence charts. *Time charts* generally use an accurate time scale whereas *sequence diagrams* do not. The *state* of a relay circuit is indicated by the combination of relays operated. On the sequence diagram the relay in an operated condition is indicated by a horizontal line. Vertical lines indicate the moment at which some action takes place, and define the *intervals*. Figure 2.1 is a sequence chart for a circuit with one *primary* (input) relay P and three *secondary relays* $A, B,$ and C.

The arrows in the diagram indicate the controlling element for each secondary relay change. Thus operating P causes A to operate. When A operates, B is operated. When P is released, C is operated, which releases A. The time chart, as opposed to a sequence diagram, looks like Fig. 2.1 except the horizontal scale is in actual time units.

Sequential circuit design proceeded by first assuming a "normal" idle state and then determining a "normal" input sequence, which took the circuit back to the "normal" idle state. When alternative input sequences could occur, these were also shown on the sequence diagram. After the number of secondary relays was determined, then control paths that caused the secondary relays to operate properly had to be developed. Secondary relays "provide a record of significant actions the circuit has taken, and thus guide future circuit operations."† Secondary relays were generally the locking (latching or holding) type; these had a normally open contact in a feedback path to its own coil.

In 1951, Keister *et al.* [4] characterized the most difficult part of sequential circuit design as determining the secondary relays required, and then determining an *operating sequence* for them (choosing suitable intervals for their operation and release). The necessity for secondary relays depends on whether "there are intervals in the sequence which have identical input combinations but require different output combinations."† This is the definition of a sequential circuit because the circuit required memory, which in their text took the form of secondary relays. "As a minimum, the number of secondary relays must be sufficient to provide a distinct combination for each identical input interval which must be recognized."† (Methods have subsequently been described in Friedman [5] where this bound for the number of feedback loops can always be achieved.)

Keister *et al.* gave several examples of developing operating sequences, and in an appendix describe specific tools for developing sequences that avoid the more common types of malfunctions. Following the operating sequence step, it is necessary to develop *control paths* which cause the relays to behave in the prescribed manner. The control paths are divided into two

---

† From W. Keister *et al.* [4], "The Design of Switching Circuits." © 1951, D. Van Nostrand Co., Inc. Reprinted by permission of Van Nostrand-Reinhold Co., New York.

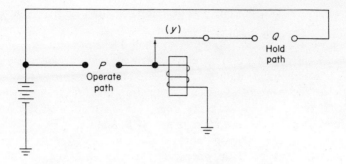

Fig. 2.2. Secondary relay control paths.

kinds: the *operate path (P)*, which energizes the secondary relay at the
proper interval, and the *hold path (Q)*, which remains closed for every interval the relay remains energized. These paths are depicted in Fig. 2.2. The
Boolean equation for y, the secondary relay, is

$$f(y) = P + yQ$$

The design of relay circuits P and Q is a combinational circuit problem:
"it is necessary only to observe what relay combinations exist during the
time the circuit path is to be closed, and to proceed by combinational
methods."† Path P must be closed during all intervals when relay y is to
move from the released to the operated state; however, from the standpoint
of relay contact minimization, path P may also be closed during any other
interval that relay y is in the operated state. The hold path Q must be
closed during any interval the relay is to be energized except possibly when
path P is closed. Two methods were suggested by Keister, Ritchie, and
Washburn for designing the hold path. First, all combinations for which the
relay must "hold" were specified and the circuit was synthesized from this
specification; second, all intervals for which the relay had to change from
the operated state to the released state were specified, and a circuit that
was open for these combinations was designed.

Once a trial circuit design was made, it had to be examined for operating
hazards, i.e., conditions under which the circuit might wind up in the wrong
state; today, this hazard is called a *steady-state hazard*. Two types of
hazards were considered [4]. The first was due to contact stagger sequences; *contact stagger* means the order in which the relay contacts are
made or broken. As a simple example, the term "make-before-break" im-

---

† From W. Keister *et al.* [4], "The Design of Switching Circuits." © 1951, D. Van Nostrand
Co., Inc. Reprinted by permission of Van Nostrand-Reinhold Co., New York.

plies both the normally open (n.o.) and normally closed (n.c.) contacts are momentarily operated during the process of energization or de-energization of the relay coil. Hazards due to contact stagger usually correspond to what today is called a *transient hazard,* although Marcus [6] has discovered situations where a steady-state hazard results. Hazards due to temporary breaks in the "hold" path can be avoided by adding circuits that are closed continuously over the successive intervals in question.

The second hazard mentioned (race condition) is now called a *critical race.* A critical race occurs when many relays are simultaneously changing and there is some relay combination that may exist momentarily and which causes a malfunction (wrong final state).

Keister, Ritchie, and Washburn did not give a systematic procedure to eliminate hazards from a circuit design, rather they pointed out the need for considerable ingenuity. They did, however, recommend the use of "legitimate sequences" (now called *totally sequential* state transitions) where only one secondary relay (or flip-flop) is to change at a time, and provided a two-dimensional relay state representation (essentially a Karnaugh map) in which these sequences could be seen as motions along vertical or horizontal line segments [4].

2. Tables of Operation

Montgomerie [7] studied the design of relay circuits and proposed the use of three states to describe the condition of a contact: (1) operated, (2) unoperated, and (3) "neutral" or between the operated and unoperated states. He defined special symbols and notation to describe the operating coil and contact positions. The interesting part of his work, however, involves the design of sequential (which he called "reflex") circuits. He introduced a "table of operations" to describe the sequence of operations. "Down the left-hand side are indicated the various possible positions of the relays comprising the circuit and the horizontal lines of the table correspond to these positions; across the top are indicated the possible positions of the external switch, α, and the columns of the Table correspond to these positions."† Using present-day terminology, each column denoted a state of the input contacts, and each row denoted a state of the normally open secondary relay contacts. Montgomerie used three values to denote the possible conditions; hence, his example which comprised one input and two secondary relays had a table of operations with three columns and nine rows. The table entry made by Montgomerie was the required state of the

† From G. A. Montgomerie [7], Sketch for an algebra of Relay and Contactor Circuits, *Proc. IEE* **95** (3), pp. 303–312. © 1948, The Institute of Electrical Engineers, London, England. Reprinted by permission.

secondary relay operating coils (either energized or de-energized) for the particular column and row condition. Thus, in 1948, Montgomerie's table of operations was a precursor to the excitation matrix defined several years later by Huffman.

B. Early Techniques for Electronic Elements

In 1952, Reed [8] discussed flip-flop operations in "synchronous Boolean machines"; i.e., in a machine where binary elements change state at discrete points of time n ($n = 1, 2, 3,\ldots$).

With time having value t, the next state of the flip-flop y_j is $y_j(t+\tau)$ or $Y_j(t)$ and is a function of the state of the flip-flops in the system at time t, that is, of $y_i(t)$ ($i = 1,\ldots,N$) and the input variables (or forcing functions) $x_i(t)$ ($i = 1,\ldots, M$). When time has discrete instances, then $y_j(t+\tau)$ may also be denoted $y_j(t+1)$.

The following system of time difference Boolean equations was termed the *synchronous Boolean system*:

$$y_j(t+1) = f_j(y_1(t), y_2(t), y_3(t),\ldots, y_N(t); x_1(t),\ldots, x_M(t))$$

where index j varies from 1 to N.

Reed proceeded to define a binary-valued "change operator" $a_j(t) = y_j(t) \oplus y_j(t+1)$ which had value 1 at time t when the next-state of flip-flop y_j was to change.† The set of change equations $a_i(t)$, $i = 1,\ldots, N$ is an equivalent representation of the time difference equations. For synthesis, a combinational circuit for $a_i(t)$ can serve as an input to a clocked complementing or toggle flip-flop in an electronic implementation of a synchronous Boolean system. Reed stated that except for some synchronization problems at the electronic level, his system of equations could represent the abstract model of a binary digital computer [8].

Reed described a three flip-flop counter by means of a truth table, where the counter next-state was a function of the present state. He derived Boolean equations for the change operators for the three flip-flops. From these equations, the counter was implemented by using AND and OR gates for the three "change operator" circuits (assuming the flip-flop complement outputs were available) and then using the change operator circuit outputs as the respective inputs to three toggle (complementing) flip-flops.

For more complex systems, sets of memory elements (called "files" by Reed) were hypothesized; in addition the possible combinational rela-

† Note that the symbol $\oplus$ denotes the exclusive-or operation.

tionships were considered so as to satisfy the desired input and output relationships of the system.

A description of the method using a system of Boolean equations was
given by Nelson [9]. This work, appearing in 1954, was delivered to the
PGEC Los Angeles Chapter in 1951. He showed how Boolean statements
described the operation of gates or combinational elements, and how a difference equation described flip-flops. As with Reed, he divided time into
discrete instants, and the flip-flop signal $y_i(t+1)$ at time $t+1$ was expressed
in terms of its present state $y_i(t)$ and present inputs $P(t)$, $R(t)$ at time t. A
truth table for the particular flip-flop as concisely described by Nelson is
shown in Table 2.1a (note that the over bar indicates Boolean negation).
The actual truth table of the function, Table 2.1b, shows the next-state
described as a function of the inputs and the present state.

The Boolean equation for this function is

$$y(t+1) = \bar{P}(t)\bar{y}(t) + R(t)y(t)$$

The described flip-flop behaves like today's JK flip-flop except J corresponds to $\bar{P}$ and K corresponds to $\bar{R}$.

In applying Boolean algebra to computer design, the processes to be
performed by the computer are listed, and each process is defined by statements specifying its logical properties. Input and output information corresponds mathematically to binary signal variables. A set of algebraic
equations describes the relationships between these variables. Nelson observed the difficulty of tracing signal paths through a maze of circuit elements in block diagrams and felt translating a verbal description into a list
of these algebraic equations was easier than going directly from the verbal
description to a block diagram [9].

TABLE 2.1.   Flip-Flop Function

(a)	Nelson's concise description		(b)	Actual truth	table	
$P(t)$	$R(t)$	$y(t+1)$	$P(t)$	$R(t)$	$y(t)$	$y(t+1)$
0	0	$\overline{y(t)}$	0	0	0	1
0	1	1	0	0	1	0
1	0	0	0	1	0	1
1	1	$y(t)$	0	1	1	1
			1	0	0	0
			1	0	1	0
			1	1	0	0
			1	1	1	1

C. The Classical Models

In the early developmental period of sequential switching theory, the importance of the concept of the internal state emerged. The importance of this concept was independently recognized by Huffman, Moore, and Kleene. The descriptive tools introduced by these researchers include: the flow table and excitation matrix by Huffman, the flow table and transition diagram by Moore, and the regular expression by Kleene. Mealy's model seems to be a modification of Moore's to accommodate a different class of memory element, and the work of Muller and Bartky represents an original approach to sequential switching circuit analysis.

1. The Huffman Model

The procedure of Keister *et al.* [4] was based on a normal sequence and did not display all possible input sequences. Further, their procedure provided no systematic method for determining secondary relays. Huffman [10] successfully attacked both of these problems by devising a *flow table*. The flow table forces the designer, during synthesis, to consider all possible input sequences; it also provides a problem statement that allows for minimizing the number of internal states required in the circuit. The Huffman flow table has generally replaced the timing chart as a starting point for formal textbook synthesis procedures. The timing chart, however, remains a valuable practical and descriptive tool. (For example, a recent textbook [11] uses it extensively, but more significant is its universal use in computer engineering manuals on logic [12].)

Huffman's work appeared in 1954 [10]. He first considered relay networks. Circuit inputs directly controlled x or *primary* relays. All other relays in the circuit were y or *secondary* relays. Each secondary relay is controlled by a network of contacts from all relays, both primary and secondary. Each state of the set of y relays is a secondary state, S_i. The outputs also result from networks of contacts of primary and secondary relays.

Huffman showed how such a circuit could be analyzed. He labeled the secondary relays $y_1, \ldots, y_s$ and output terminals $z_1, \ldots, z_g$. Each y and z network is a function of the *total state*, i.e., the x relay (input) state and y relay (internal) state; and as such a table of combinations can be made for each network. By rewriting the table with the input states as columns and the y (internal) states as rows, the Y and Z matrices are formed. The Y-matrix entry for a total state is the excitation function or next state for the y relays and the Z-matrix entry is the output state. If the next internal state entry is the same as the present state (row), the total state is *stable*;

otherwise it is *transient*. Huffman pointed out a problem that might exist in the Y matrix: a critical race exists if two or more secondary relays are simultaneously changing state and the final state (outcome of the transition) is not independent of the individual operate and release times of the relays involved.

Huffman notes that changes in state of the y relays are vertical movements in the Y matrix whereas a change in input state is a horizontal movement. For example, in Fig. 2.3a, with secondary relays y_1, y_2 unoperated (row 00) and inputs x_1 in the 0-state and x_2 in the 1-state (column 01), then the input change x_1 going to the 1-state causes a horizontal movement in row 00 to column 11. The entry 10 in this total state means that y_1 is to change to the 1-state and y_2 is to remain in the 0-state, indicating a vertical movement within column 11 to row 10. Once a stable total state is reached, only a change in the input state (horizontal movement) will cause further changes. Huffman also permitted the secondary relays to cycle indefinitely (oscillate), provided the output state remained constant, i.e., if the circuit displayed "ultimately stable terminal action."

Huffman converted the Y matrix to a *flow table* by first assigning an integer to each stable total state and circling the stable total state entries (Fig. 2.3b). The uncircled entries tell which next state results if the circuit is placed in the total state in question. A flow table is *normal* if the next state for each transient state is a stable state. If the next state of at least one transient state is a transient state, the flow table is *nonnormal*. The flow table of Fig. 2.3 is normal. Flow tables with oscillations have not been thoroughly investigated.

Circuits for which the synthesis procedure of Huffman apply have the following restriction: *the input state can be changed only when the ultimately stable terminal action is reached.* Also, to avoid multiple-input change problems, it is assumed the input state is changed one variable at a

y_1 y_2	x_1 x_2 00	01	11	10
0 0	00	00	10	10
0 1	01	00	10	11
1 1	01	11	11	11
1 0	00	10	10	10

(a)

y_1 y_2	x_1 x_2 00	01	11	10
0 0	①	②	8	9
0 1	③	2	8	6
1 1	3	④	⑤	⑥
1 0	1	⑦	⑧	⑨

(b)

Fig. 2.3. Huffman flow table from Y matrix. (a) Y matrix. (b) Flow table.

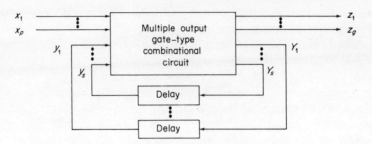

Fig. 2.4.   Huffman model for gate-type realization.

time. The first step of the synthesis procedure is to convert the problem statement to a flow table. After the number of rows in the flow table is minimized, secondary relay states are assigned to the flow table rows. This assignment must avoid critical races because the operate and release times of the relays are assumed to vary, and races cannot be guaranteed to end in ties. Huffman recommended first changing one Y relay at a time, then reconsidering where noncritical races could be allowed. Another assumption Huffman made was that the inertial delay or "response time" of the relays exceeded the "hazard time" (worst-case delay) of the combinational switching network analogous to the P and Q paths of Fig. 2.2. Thus the inertia of the relay, working in favor of the designer, "rode out" switching spikes or transients in the combinational portion of the network.

Once the Y matrix is made critical-race-free, the Z matrix is filled in. These matrices represent truth tables for combinational circuits for the outputs. Thus, given a single sequential circuit problem involving, for example, three secondary relays and two outputs, Huffman's procedure converts it to five combinational circuit problems. As Reed converted a clocked sequential circuit to several combinational circuits, Huffman did the same for unclocked sequential circuits.

Huffman's work was based on relay technology, but the method was general enough that he proceeded to relate his procedure to gate-type switching circuits. The flow table specification, and state assignment without critical races, do not depend on relay implementations. The resulting combinational circuit specifications called for by the Y matrix could be implemented just as well by gate-type (as opposed to relay contact) AND, OR, and NOT logic elements. The output of a gate-type combinational circuit for the ith secondary variable is designated Y_i. This signal, in the general case, is passed through a delay (to represent the time lag between relay excitation and response) and becomes an input signal designated Y_i. (Huffman points out that in many cases this delay element is not necessary for proper operation.) The analogy with relay circuits, continues Huffman, is that corresponding to the device (a relay), is a *secondary delay location*. The feedback loops of gate-type circuits also need a gain that is greater than unity. Figure 2.4 shows Huffman's model [10] for "electronic" circuits. This concept, where the feedback loops have delay elements, is now called the feedback-delay model.

The essential points of Huffman's model are that due to circuit delays, races in internal state variables are not assumed always to end in ties, and that once a stable condition has been attained, only an input state change can cause further state changes. The input signals are not pulses unless the circuit has attained a stable condition before the "pulse" returns to zero. There is no predetermined time at which inputs change, and more than one input could change at a time, provided it did so within a given time span.

In describing his model and synthesis procedure, Huffman addressed the engineering problems of gate (or relay operate and release) delays in the circuit. A *steady-state hazard* with respect to a given input transition exists in the circuit if stray delays cause the response (final stable condition) to be other than the predicted or desired response. In the case of relay circuits with large inertial relay delays, the critical race was felt to be the only cause for steady-state hazards until Marcus [6] proved otherwise. However, with the advent of electronic circuits, and the assumption that interconnection (line) delays could be the same order of magnitude as gate delays, malfunctions may be caused by several gate delays racing a line delay. Eichelberger describes an elegant procedure called ternary analysis which detects all such steady-state hazards [13]. One particular malfunction that may occur in gate-type sequential circuits, unless suitable delays are purposely inserted in the circuit, is called an *essential hazard* by Unger [14]. The essential hazard is a property of the behavioral description and not the structural description of the circuit; i.e., a circuit may be hazardfree even though its flow table contains an "essential hazard." If there exists a stable state S_0 and binary input variable x such that starting in S_0, three successive input changes in x bring the system to a state other than one arrived at after the first change in x, then the behavioral description has an essential hazard. What can happen with the essential hazard, unless the circuit is properly designed, is that one portion of the circuit changes in response to the input change, and a second part of the circuit "sees" the secondary response before it "sees" the initial input change. This second part of the circuit may erroneously initiate a change; the net result is the response to three changes in input x, instead of just one. Recently, general synthesis procedures have been developed which avoid this problem when the magnitude of line delays are suitably constrained [15, 16]. When line delays may be arbitrarily large, however, the essential hazard is the fundamental limitation to sequential circuit synthesis [17].

In summarizing his synthesis procedure, Huffman lists eight steps, which are paraphrased below:

(1) Specify the problem in terms of a flow table.

(2) Check the flow table for conciseness.

(3) Shorten the flow table, if possible, through "row merges."

(4) Make a secondary state assignment.

(5) Develop a τ matrix. (A τ matrix indicates which secondary relays are to change; this function corresponds to what Reed called $a_i(t)$. Huffman suggested that only one secondary relay change at a time in order to avoid critical races.)

(6) Derive a Y matrix corresponding to the τ matrix. (The Y matrix describes the excitation function for each secondary relay.)

(7) Develop the Z matrix. (The Z matrix describes the excitation function for the output relays.)

(8) Note that the Y and Z matrices describe combinational circuits which realize the flow table.

Step 1, of course, remains the most difficult step in practice. Steps 2 and 3 are called flow table reduction, state reduction, or state minimization. Steps 4 and 5 comprise the state assignment problem. Steps 6, 7, and 8 are generally simple mechanical procedures.

2. The Moore Model

Moore's [2] model of a sequential machine, which appeared in 1956, specifically assumes a finite number of input symbols (or input states), internal states, and output symbols (or output states). The present internal state depends on the previous input state and internal state, and the present output state depends only on the present internal state. The behavior of such a machine may be deduced by feeding it input symbols and observing the output symbols.

> Time is assumed to come in discrete steps, so the machine can be thought of as a synchronous device. Since many of the component parts of actual automata have variable speeds, this assumption means the theory has not been stated in the most general terms. In practice, some digital computers and most telephone central offices have been designed asynchronously. However, by providing a central "clock" source of uniform time intervals it is possible to organize even

asynchronous components so that they act in the discrete time steps of a synchronous machine.†

Thus Moore was not concerned with steady-state hazards. Moore described the internal behavior by two equivalent means: a table and a transition diagram. Although Moore's work was independent of Huffman's work, the table for the machine is similar to Huffman's flow table except that the rows are "previous" states, the columns are "previous" inputs, and the entry is the "present" state (Fig. 2.5). The form of Huffman's flow table, defined in terms of the "present" state and "next" state, is the form which is now prevalent.

A point of difference between the state transitions described by a Huffman or Moore flow table is that in Moore's table, as Krieger [18] notes, all states are equally stable because each lasts for an interval between clock pulses, and transitions are one-step transitions. The notion of the "operating point" [19] passing through intermediate transient states, as in Huffman's Y matrix, is absent in this model. Furthermore, due to the clock signal, one input state can follow itself in an input sequence, a notion which is absent in the Huffman model. In his paper, Moore [2] did not concern himself with the realization of the model; he was more interested in behavioral analysis and state equivalence.

Moore introduced an alternative description of circuit behavior, which he called a *transition diagram*. The transition diagram (also called state diagram or flow diagram) for Fig. 2.5 is shown in Fig. 2.6. The nodes

Present state

Previous state	Previous input		Previous state	Present output
	0	1		
S_1	S_1	S_3	S_1	0
S_2	S_1	S_3	S_2	0
S_3	S_4	S_4	S_3	0
S_4	S_2	S_2	S_4	1

Fig. 2.5. Moore machine description.

† From E. F. Moore [2], Gedanken Experiments on Sequential Machines. *Annals of Mathematics Studies,* No. 34. © 1956, Princeton Univ. Press, Princeton, New Jersey. Reprinted by permission.

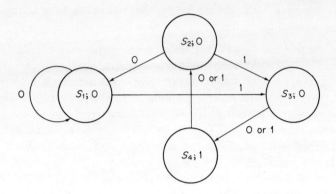

Fig. 2.6.   Transition diagram for Fig. 2.5.

represent states and their outputs. The arrows between the states show the input which sends the machine from the previous state (tail of the arrow) to the present state (head of the arrow).

3. *The Mealy Model*

Although the word *asynchronous* does not appear in Huffman's work, both Moore and Mealy referred to Huffman's model as such and referred to their own models as *synchronous*. Mealy noted that Huffman's synthesis procedure did not apply directly to clocked circuits (e.g., those used in the SEAC) [20, 21] and amended the procedure so that it applied to his model [22].

Mealy said, "It is very tempting at the outset to make the flat statement: There is no such thing as a synchronous circuit."† This would be true, he went on, if a synchronous circuit were defined such that no *physical* circuit satisfied the criteria. However, "the engineer does recognize a certain class of circuits which he calls synchronous. The unfortunate fact is that the distinction between a synchronous and an asynchronous circuit is very hazy in many cases of actual engineering interest."† Mealy gave some guidelines, however, in describing a synchronous circuit: (1) the circuit is pulse-input, pulse-output, these pulses occuring in synchronism with timing pulses from a clock, and (2) the clock rate may be varied within limits. Mealy did not restrict the input pulses to occur only one at a time; any combination of pulse or no-pulse could occur on the input lines at clock pulse time.

Mealy's set of building blocks included combinational gate elements and

† From G. H. Mealy [22], A Method for Synthesizing Sequential Circuits. *Bell Syst. Tech. J.* **34**, pp. 1045–1079, © 1955. Reprinted by permission.

a unit delay. Specific reference is made to SEAC type circuits [20, 21]. However, while the SEAC used a four-phase clock, Mealy assumed single-phase operation. The model is similar to Moore's except Mealy's output is a pulse and may depend on the present input as well as the present internal state. The next-state (i.e., state of the excitation variables Y_i) is a function of the present state variables y_j and present input variables x_k. Each excitation variable signal line Y_i is connected as input to a unit delay, and the unit delay output is a present state variable y_i. Mealy's model is shown in Fig. 2.7 and is similar to Fig. 2.4 in that it uses the feedback-delay concept.

In relating his work to Huffman's, Mealy notes in asynchronous circuits "(1) that no clock will be used, and (2) that '1' in switching algebra will correspond to a high voltage or current, an energized relay coil, or operated relay contacts."† Mealy also notes the possibility of cyclic behavior in asynchronous circuits, and that therefore the same truth table cannot, in general, be used for both a synchronous and asynchronous realization of a given circuit. "The reason for this is tied very closely with the fact that we speak of presence or absence of pulses in synchronous circuits but of quasi-steady-state conditions on leads in asynchronous circuits."† Thus, the Mealy or Moore flow table is interpreted differently from the Huffman flow table. In the Mealy–Moore flow table, the row and column entries denote conditions during the time designated "presence of pulses." The table entry denotes the next-state, which is stored on the delay line during the "spacer" period of time designated "absence of pulses." It is this "spacer" state, not explicitly shown on the flow table, which permits an input state to succeed itself in an input sequence to a synchronous circuit (i.e., which permits "like successive inputs," so called by Cadden [19]). In the case of a Huffman flow table, if such a spacer input existed, it would have to appear as a column (or columns) in the flow table because all input signals (or states) are explicit. Mealy also proposed a transition diagram (which he called a state diagram) similar to Moore's however, the output state is associated with the transition between internal states rather than with the internal state itself. (Huffman also associated the output with the total state.) These distinctions are later considered in more detail, where Cadden's work is reviewed.

The Mealy model then assumes the existence of a clock and pulse signals. Mealy identifies "asynchronous" as "no clock" and the dc coupling of level signals. Yet the similarities in the synthesis procedures are many. Mealy adopted and improved upon the very similar Huffman and Moore‡

† From G. H. Mealy [22], A Method for Synthesizing Sequential Circuits. *Bell Syst. Tech. J.* **34**, pp. 1045–1079, © 1955. Reprinted by permission.

‡ Although Mealy's paper appeared in print before Moore's, Mealy was aware of, and specifically referenced, Moore's work.

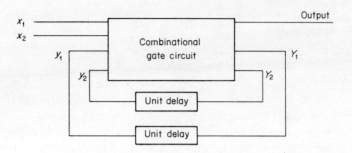

Fig. 2.7.   The Mealy model.

procedures for state reduction at the flow table level. The notion of the Y matrix to specify the excitation functions carries over into Mealy's work. What the synchronous model did, however, was to specify external timing considerations such that all secondary variable races ended in ties, thus eliminating the critical race problem. Another similarity between Mealy and Huffman is use of the combinational network for the excitation functions, with feedback through delays, as demonstrated by the similarity between Figs. 2.4 and 2.7. (This model of sequential circuits was called the "feedback-delay" concept by Caldwell [23].) In the case of Huffman, the delay may be the inertial delay of a relay which is not precise whereas in Mealy's case the delay is precise.

   Mealy summarized his synthesis procedure in five steps, which are paraphrased below:

   (1) Write a transition diagram or flow table.
   (2) Obtain a reduced flow table.
   (3) Make the state assignment. (For asynchronous realizations this must be free of races.)
   (4) Write the circuit equations.
   (5) Design the combinational circuit.

   Mealy notes that his method is pertinent to synchronous as well as asynchronous circuits; however, he adds that "the basic concepts of Huffman's paper are valid in both cases."† In commenting on his synthesis procedure, Mealy states: "unfortunately, the initial step in the process relies heavily on the designer's ingenuity."† Regarding the second step, he comments: "using a minimum number of storage elements is not always

---

† From G. H. Mealy [22], A Method for Synthesizing Sequential Circuits. *Bell Syst. Tech. J.* **34**, pp. 1045–1079, © 1955. Reprinted by permission.

wise. In practical situations, the choice of components dictate one's criterion for minimality, and this criterion must ultimately be based on considerations of economy and reliability."† Mealy also provides insight into the usefulness of such a systematic procedure. ,

> It is probably fair to say that the theory furnishes, at present at least, only generalized methods of attack on synthesis together with a small handfull of particularized tools for design. It is the author's belief that these methods are genuinely useful insofar as they aid in understanding the nature of sequential circuits and furnish a unified way of thinking about circuits during their design. It would be a mistake, however, to believe that they provide detailed design methods in the same sense in which such methods are available for electrical network synthesis.†

Mealy's points are valid today.

4. The Speed Independent Model

Muller and Bartky of the University of Illinois were interested in the self-timed or unclocked philosophy of system timing employed in the IAS computer [24]. Two computers, the ORDVAC and Illiac I, were built at the University of Illinois and patterned after the IAS computer. Some of the completion signals of the design, e.g., the 12-microsecond delay for the adder, depended on a fixed upper bound on the gate switching times. The speed-independent theory [24], assumes no upper bound on gate switching times; also, there is no assumption constraining the relative delays between gates.

The state of the circuit is described by the set of signal values at various points in the circuit. If this definition is specialized to binary signals for our purposes, then we may assume the circuit states are described by the binary value at each gate output. The gate is in equilibrium if its output is consistent with its inputs (e.g., an AND gate is in equilibrium if its output is in the 1-state and none of its inputs is in the 0-state). A gate not in equilibrium is *excited*. Input changes to a circuit generally result in one or more excited gates. Although Muller assumed interconnection delays were zero, a one-input "dummy" gate could be placed in particular interconnections of interest to simulate the delay [25]. Gate delays were assumed to be inertial; i.e., if an excited gate were to lose its excitation before its output changed, the output would not subsequently change.

To determine the possible behavior of the circuit, Muller and Bartky constructed a directed graph. If state S_1 is the initial state (which results

† From G. H. Mealy [22], A Method for Synthesizing Sequential Circuits. *Bell Syst. Tech. J.* **34**, 1045–1079, © 1955. Reprinted by permission.

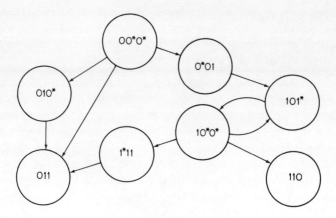

Fig. 2.8. An allowed sequence graph.

from an input change) and state S_2 is the result of one or more (some combination) of excited gates in S_1 going simultaneously to equilibrium, then an arrow is drawn from S_1 to S_2. This process may be repeated until all combinations of changes are represented on the graph. An *allowed sequence* of total states results from starting at S_1 and following the arrows until either a stable state is reached or a "terminal class" (loop) of states (as in an oscillation) is reached. An allowed sequence graph is shown in Fig. 2.8. Excited gates are denoted by the asterisk superscript. The circuit whose graph is depicted is not speed independent with respect to state 000 because there are three terminal classes: (011), (110), and (100,101).

Some oscillations, called psuedo-terminal classes, are disallowed as terminal classes if, in order to sustain the oscillation indefinitely, a gate must remain indefinitely in the same excited state. This is a direct consequence of the assumption that although gate delays do not have an upper bound, they are finite. The circuit is *speed-independent* with respect to state S_1 if the allowed sequences from S_1 have the same terminal class. The circuit may be similarly analyzed for all transitions of interest. This specialization of speed-independent theory can be linked to Huffman's work by defining a circuit-derived Y matrix [17]. Here one considers each gate output as a y variable (internal state variable) and constructs the corresponding Y matrix. Thus from a behavioral viewpoint of a binary-valued switching circuit, the Huffman Y matrix is no more or less general than the behavioral description used in speed-independent theory.

A speed-independent circuit is *semimodular* if, whenever a gate becomes excited, it cannot lose its excitation until the gate changes state. In other words, once a gate G becomes excited, subsequent allowed changes in other gates in the circuit do not cause a change in the inputs to G such that G is no longer excited. This implies that if the gate delays are pure in nature, the circuit will behave as expected. Muller has proved an interconnection theorem for semimodular circuits. This theorem deals with reply back signals and can be applied to both serial and parallel interconnections of semimodular circuits.

As previously noted, the Illiac I, an asynchronous computer, was modeled after the IAS computer. The Illiac II was also asynchronous, but had a firmer theoretical footing. To this end, sections of the machine were built according to the speed-independent theory. Swartwout [26] describes the method used for the arithmetic controls. The general controls were laid out in flow chart form, where each flow chart block described some actions such as gating data into registers and setting or clearing control flip-flops. The total flow chart problem was implemented by interconnecting elements chosen from a comprehensive set of basic logic diagrams, or BLDs. (The technique is not unlike that of the Digital Equipment Corporation's use of Register Transfer Modules in their "do-it-yourself" PDP-16 Module set.) Swartwout included and described ten of the most commonly used basic logic diagrams [26]. The control is described as coming close to being speed-independent, but not quite. Some feedback reply signals required large fan-out; whenever a fan-out tree was used, the speed-independent property was lost. Miller [25] devotes a chapter to describing speed-independence thoroughly, including the interconnection theorem, a flow chart approach to design, and practical problems dealing with stray delays.

5. The Finite State Automata Model

Kleene used the term *finite automata* in 1951 and did some very basic early work in this field [27]. This work is difficult to read partly because it is based on the terminology of McCulloch–Pitts Nerve Nets [28]. Moore's use of the term *finite automata* meant that the machine had "a finite number of states, a finite number of possible input symbols, and a finite number of possible output symbols," and "that the present state of a machine depends only on its previous input and previous state, and the present output depends only on its present state."†

Automata theorists often view the sequential machine as a transducer device which maps input sequences into output sequences. The input sequence is a finite string of symbols drawn from the input alphabet (set of input

† From E. F. Moore [2], Gedanken Experiments on Sequential Machines. *Annals of Mathematical Studies,* No. 34. © Princeton Univ. Press, Princeton, New Jersey. Reprinted by permission.

states). The output sequence is a finite string of symbols drawn from the output alphabet (set of output states). Between each input symbol is the null input; thus, adjacent input symbols may be the same and are distinguished by the time of occurrence. Like successive inputs and like successive outputs are permitted. In the Mealy model, adjacent output symbols are also separated by the null symbol, and the output sequence is the same length as the input sequence. In the Moore model, the output sequence may contain one more symbol than the input sequence because the output corresponding to the initial state appears prior to the arrival of the first input symbol.

In 1959, Rabin and Scott [29] specialized the output alphabet to a "yes" or "no" for the purpose of classifying *tapes*, where a tape is a finite sequence of input symbols presented to the automaton. The automaton's behavior is important: "We are not concerned with how the machine is built, but with what it can do. . . . The simple method of obtaining generality without unnecessary detail is to use the concept of *internal states*. No matter how many wires or tubes or relays the machine contains, its operation is determined by stable states of the machine at discrete time intervals."†
When the automaton is used in this way to classify tapes, it is called an *acceptor*.

The set of tapes accepted by a finite-state machine can conveniently be described by a *regular expression*. Regular expressions were first described by Kleene [27] and subsequently studied by many others. A regular expression denotes a set of input tapes. The machine's input alphabet is operated on by three operators: concatenation, the Boolean or ($+$), and star (*). Each input symbol (e.g., I_1, I_2) is a regular expression, denoting a tape of length 1. The "empty tape" (of length 0) is also a regular expression. If A and B are regular expressions, then so is AB (concatenation), $A + B$ (Boolean or), and $A*$ (star). The star operation $A*$ denotes the following set of tapes: the empty tape (called lambda), tape A, tape AA (tape A "spliced" to tape A), AAA, $AAAA$, etc.

A regular expression implies a sequential machine with a particular internal state structure; i.e., for a regular expression there exists a procedure for constructing the state transition diagram or flow table. Conversely, for a given state transition diagram, there exists a regular expression. These results are from the work of Kleene [27]. Recall, however, that unless the given finite state machine has only two output states, only the internal state structure is implied by a regular expression.

† From M. O. Rabin and D. Scott [29], Finite Automata and Their Decision Problems. *IBM J. Res. Develop.* 3 (2), pp. 114–125. © 1959, IBM Corp. Reprinted by permission.

The employment of regular expressions to avoid the use of a flow table in synthesis is described, for example, by Johnson and Lackey [30]. Here a procedure for converting a regular expression to a state transition diagram is used. A method for generating a state table for a sequential machine from regular expressions is given by Booth [31]. He extends the method to a multiple-output machine.

The Mealy model as described by a flow table, is often viewed abstractly as a 5-tuple (I, S, Z, f, g). The 5-tuple presents no more information than a flow table; however, automata theorists find it convenient to use in formulating the machine. Thus the descriptive and theoretical tools of abstract algebra may be applied to automata theory. The five components of the 5-tuple are (1) the set of inputs I, (2) the set of states S, (3) the set of outputs Z, (4) the next-state function f that maps each total state (each input and state pair) into a next state, and (5) the output function g that maps each total state to an output. Note that corresponding to each such 5-tuple there is a Mealy flow table. Similarly, note that a Moore or a Huffman flow table may also be described by a 5-tuple.

The next state function f is often represented as $f\colon S \times I \to S$. The set $S \times I$ is the Cartesian product of sets S and I. Viewing the set I as flow table columns and the set S as flow table rows, the set $S \times I$ is the set of total states, or set of squares in the flow table. Similarly, the output function g is denoted $g\colon S \times I \to Z$. This brief description shows that success in relating automata theory to existing branches of mathematics is accompanied by increased attention to terminology and notation.

D. The Later Models

In this section some variations, refinements, and improved techniques based upon the classical models are covered.

1. Autosynchronous Circuits

An interesting "speed-independent" logic and timing scheme, called autosynchronous, was described by Sims and Gray [32] in 1958. In this scheme, each binary input A is represented by two complementary signal lines, called a and a', i.e., A is converted to a two-line signal. A binary value of 1 is assigned to A when line a is in the 1-state and a' is in the 0-state; and A is assigned value 0 when a is in the 0-state and a' is in the 1-state. Circuits which operate on two-line signals may be constructed from conventional binary logic elements. Two-line (also called two-rail) AND and OR gates using single-line gates are shown in Fig. 2.9.

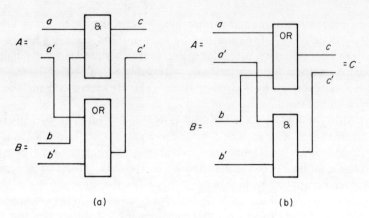

Fig. 2.9. Two-line (a) AND and (b) OR gates.

The "double-line trick" was originally devised by von Neumann [33] to demonstrate that conventional AND and OR gates were sufficient to synthesize Boolean functions and that a single-line inverter element was not needed. The reason for this is shown in Fig. 2.10, where the two-line NOT element is simply a crossing over of the two wires. A two-rail latch composed of three, four-input NOR elements appears in Maley and Earle [34]. This has three states, and thus is a *tri-state* flip-flop.

Sims and Gray adapted the two-line notation into a sequential switching system for the purpose of eliminating "spikes" ("glitches") or hazards in an unclocked (time-dependent) environment. The "spacer" or "nothing" value exists on signal A when both complementary lines a and a' are in the 0-state. All gates operate in a "return-to-nothing" mode. Each input state to the system is followed by the null or spacer state, causing all gate outputs to go to the nothing state. With the circuit initially at "nothing," a job completion signal ("return to nothing") can be achieved following presentation of a valid input state by detecting a valid signal on each output pair. This signals for an input spacer state. The signal that the circuit is again ready for the next input state ("send new input") is achieved by detecting all output pairs in the nothing state. A problem arises in using this scheme to implement sequential switching circuits. A memory element output, to be significant, is a valid signal. A valid signal combined with a nothing signal in a two-line AND or OR gate may give a valid signal or a nothing signal on the output. This may result in premature completion signals unless steps are taken to avoid the problem.

In Sims and Gray the two-line scheme is used in transferring data from one register to the next. The sending register is cleared to "nothing" after

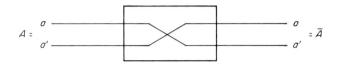

Fig. 2.10. A two-rail NOT element.

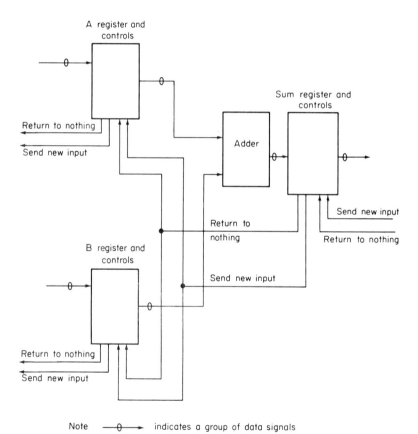

Note ───0─→ indicates a group of data signals

Fig. 2.11. Autosynchronous adder.

its data have been passed to the next stage. An autosynchronous adder scheme is shown in Fig. 2.11. In a paper by Muller [35] speed-independent theory is combined with the two-line notation to achieve reply signals at the gate level. That is, each AND or OR gate circuit sends reply signals to each circuit that provides it with inputs. Subsequently Hammel [36] applied Muller's results at the sequential circuit level. The use of the two-rail encoding to achieve a completion signal in sequential circuits where gate delays may become arbitrarily large is also discussed in Armstrong *et al.* [37]. Maley and Earle [34] suggest the two-line trick might be most efficiently employed in combination with more conventional techniques (e.g., the implementation of the carry signal in a parallel adder).

2. Clocked Circuits

Phister's book, which appeared in 1958, presented a detailed treatment of design procedures utilizing flip-flops (as opposed to the feedback delay model) which received early contributions from Reed and Nelson, and was further developed by many West-Coast machine designers [3]. Phister describes procedures for clocked systems; however, his memory elements were flip-flops instead of delay units. Mealy's procedure was thus modified to arrive at flip-flop input equations rather than an equation describing the input to a delay element. Phister assumed that all memory element inputs were gated with clock pulses, and that changes took place between clock pulses such that only the high and low voltage levels of the flip-flops and combinational circuit outputs had any effect. Thus, except possibly the clock pulse, the inputs are levels and not pulses.

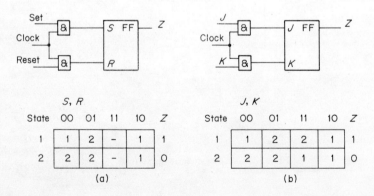

Fig. 2.12. (a) Clocked set-reset flip-flop and Moore flow table. (b) Clocked *JK* flip-flop and Moore flow table.

Phister showed that by adding suitable logic, it was possible to make one kind of clocked memory element look like another. Thus his approach adapted the synchronous flow tables and procedures to clocked circuits with level inputs and level outputs; i.e., circuits like those found in the IBM 702 and 705 computers [38].

Two popular flip-flops described by Phister are the clocked set–reset (SR) flip-flop and the clocked (three-input) *JK* flip-flop (Fig. 2.12). The set–reset flip-flop has the state transition undefined when both the set and reset inputs are in the 1-state at clock pulse time. The *JK* flip-flop behaves in a manner similar to the SR flip-flop with the exception that when both the *J* and *K* inputs are in the 1-state the flip-flop will "toggle" (complement), i.e., change state, as shown in the flow table of Fig. 2.12b.

The "clock-pulse AND" gates are described by Phister only once; all subsequent memory element drawings and Boolean equations appear without the clock signal but "with the understanding that a clock-pulse 'and' circuit is included somewhere."† This particular method of adding timing signals is considered synchronous and is often called "gating level signals against a clock."

Phister observed that the logic designer's job was often described in vague terms; this gave him so much leeway that no invariant set of rules for design was possible. He points out that certain design methods could be used, nevertheless. Phister describes the Huffman–Mealy–Moore method of state reduction, but he (like Mealy) points out that minimizing memory elements without regard to gates ignores an important aspect of the minimization problem. Further, the method does not work for incompletely specified problems, nor does it help the state assignment problem. It remains, however, a useful simplification tool.

Phister used the same basic steps for synthesis as did Huffman and Mealy, but since he did not use the feedback-delay model, he obtained the excitation equations in a slightly different manner. The Y matrix specifies, for an internal state variable y_i, when its next value Y_i is the 1-state. From the Y matrix a Boolean equation is derived that describes the next value for each state variable in terms of the present state variable and input state values. Phister stated that as these equations described the application of a particular flip-flop, they were called "application equations" [3]. If delay flip-flops are used as memory elements, then the application equations also describe the flip-flop inputs.

If a state variable is associated with a set–reset flip-flop, then of greater

---

† From M. Phister [3], "Logical Design of Digital Computers." © 1958, John Wiley and Sons, New York. Reprinted by permission.

Control and timing		Input equations (flip flop Y)	
Time	$C_1 C_2$	J_Y	K_Y
–	00	$\overline{B}$	$BC + \overline{B}\overline{C} + BX$
–	01	X	$\overline{X}$
–	10	0	0
–	11	0	1

Fig. 2.13. Truth table outlining the function of flip-flop Y.

interest than the application equations are the conditions for setting or resetting the flip-flop. Therefore, Phister gave a procedure for deriving the flip-flop *input equations* from the application equations. Marcus [39] gives an excellent general procedure for obtaining input equations for many types of flip-flops.

In Chapter 11, Phister gives an overview of the design process. The following five steps briefly describe the process:

(a) *Establishment of a framework.* This step generally concerns splitting up the system into functional units and defining the interfaces between the units.

(b) *Provision of a word description.* This means a detailed description of how functional units work together, including a definition of what operations take place at each step, and source and destination information for each data transfer.

(c) *Formation of truth tables.* For this step the designer translates a functional unit's word description into a series of truth tables. Phister performs this step by an example [3]. Essentially, a column or columns are provided for some control but primarily for timing information. Each row for these columns represents a different machine time. For each row, the input conditions for each flip-flop input is written as a Boolean statement. A truth table example, shown in Fig. 2.13, is a simplified version of Phister's Table 6-19 [3]. (The format is of interest here; the function performed in Fig. 2.13 is meaningless.) In this example, *JK* flip-flop Y is independent of which clock pulse (timing) is used as indicated by the dashes in the first column. From the second row of Fig. 2.13 it is seen that when input signals C_1 and C_2 are 0 and 1 respectively, the logic designer wishes flip-flop Y to assume the value of signal X. When C_1 and C_2 are 10 (third row), flip-flop Y remains unchanged. Flip-flop Y is reset when C_1C_2 is 11.

(d) *Derivation of input equations.* This procedure is straightforward; a

Boolean equation is written for each flip-flop input from the truth table. Listed below are the equations for Fig. 2.13.

$$J_Y = \bar{C}_1\bar{C}_2\bar{B} + \bar{C}_1C_2X$$
$$K_Y = \bar{C}_1\bar{C}_2(BC + \bar{B}\bar{C} + BX) + \bar{C}_1C_2\bar{X} + C_1C_2$$

(e) *Revision and rearrangement.* Here, a comprehensive review of the computer design might cause a completely new arrangement.

This procedure is analogous to the symbolic method of design described in Chapter 3, where the lines of the "truth table" correspond to micro-operations.

3. Pulsed Sequential Circuits

In the introduction to Chapter 15 of his book, published in 1958, Professor Caldwell [23] of MIT made the following commentary:

> High-speed, digital computing machines, with their sensational advances in design and in application, offer eloquent testimony to the power of the pulse. In this chapter we extend the concepts and methods we have developed for the synthesis of sequential circuits using levels to represent variables, to the design of circuits in which variables are represented by pulses. There are many types of pulse circuits, using many types of components. Our objective in this discussion is to establish principles and methods that are sufficiently powerful and flexible to be applicable and effective in any pulse switching situation.†

Since Caldwell was at MIT, it is interesting to observe how well the model fits the circuit family used in Whirlwind I (built by MIT) and SAGE.

The properties of the model are listed below:

(1) All inputs and outputs are pulses. (Level signals are also permitted, but only as internal state variables.)

(2) The shapes of input pulses and their durations are assumed to be compatible with the components and circuits used.

(3) There must be a minimum time interval between successive pulses, called the circuit *resolution time.*

(4) The output pulses occur simultaneously with the input pulse but

---

† From S. H. Caldwell [23], "Switching Circuits and Logical Design." © 1959, John Wiley and Sons, New York. Reprinted by permission.

$$x_1, \; x_2, \; x_3$$

000	100	010	001	Z
①	2	4	5	0
3	②	–	–	0
③	7	8	5	0
1	–	④	–	0
6	–	–	⑤	0
⑥	2	4	5	0
6	⑦	–	–	0
3	–	⑧	–	1

(a)

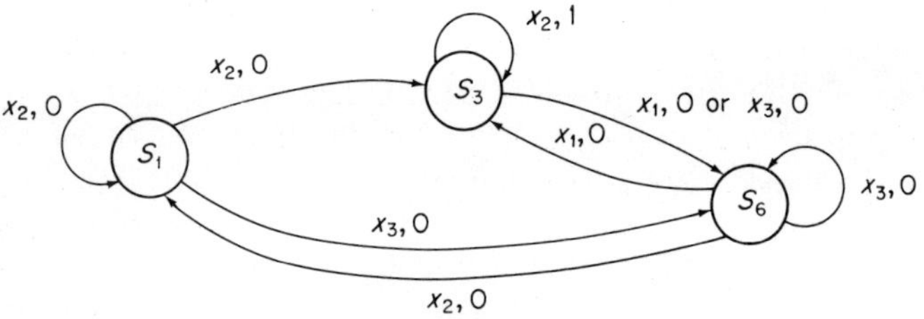

(b)

	x_1	x_2	x_3
S_1	$S_3, 0$	$S_1, 0$	$S_6, 0$
S_3	$S_6, 0$	$S_3, 1$	$S_6, 0$
S_6	$S_3, 0$	$S_1, 0$	$S_6, 0$

(c)

Fig. 2.14. Behavioral descriptions of a pulsed sequential circuit. (a) A flow table with pulses treated as changes of level. (b) A state transition diagram. (c) Mealy flow table.

otherwise no other pulses are to occur simultaneously. (Only a single input pulse occurs at a time.)

Caldwell showed that the pulse could be viewed as two level changes; therefore, a Huffman flow table could be drawn to describe any pulsed sequential circuit. Such a flow table, he notes, has many unspecified entries because following the pulse input state, the input can only return to the "all zero" (spacer) state. In addition, no flow table columns need to be provided for input states with more than one input signal in the 1-state, since this is not allowed. Such a flow table appears in Fig. 2.14a.

Caldwell next showed that the flow table could be converted to a transition diagram. The states of the diagram are those of the spacer column. Assume the flow table is in state 1 and goes to state 3 by a transition of input signal x_1 from 0 to 1, followed by x_1 going back to 0. This action is represented on the transition diagram as a single transition from state 1 to state 3. The output accompanying the transition is the output according to the flow table which occurs when x_1 is in the 1-state. Caldwell thus obtained a transition diagram for a circuit conforming to the Mealy model; the step to a Mealy flow table from the transition diagram is simple and straightforward (Fig. 2.14). It is an equally simple matter to reverse the order of these steps.

For memory elements, Caldwell considered toggle (τ) flip-flops (a pulse on the single input causes the output to change state following the response time) and the set–reset flip-flop. These flip-flops were assumed to provide dc or level outputs. To synthesize circuits, it is necessary to combine the level signals with the pulse signals. This is accomplished by an AND gate which passes a pulse input if the level inputs are in the 1-state [23]; the analogy with the Whirlwind I pentode gated pulse amplifier should be readily seen.

Caldwell, like Phister, noted that by the addition of suitable gating, one type of flip-flop could be made to look like another [23]. The synthesis procedure consists of writing a flow-table, assigning secondary states to flow table rows, and preparing an excitation matrix. Since the pulse durations are short compared to the flip-flop response times, the state assignment is arbitrary and can possibly be made to minimize gating circuitry.

To demonstrate the breadth of application of the basic concepts, Caldwell applied the method to the two-phase magnetic-core logic technology. To emphasize the output function need not entirely consist of pulses, his problem 15.8 has voltage-level outputs specified.

4. The Fundamental Mode and Pulse Mode Models

McCluskey [40] characterized the Moore model as being pulse input and level output, and characterized the Mealy model as being pulse input and pulse output. Sequential circuits with at least one pulse input were called *pulse mode* circuits, regardless of the type of output signal. Huffman's model assumed level inputs, level outputs, and the inputs were not changed until the circuit had reached a stable condition. McCluskey said these circuits operated in *fundamental mode* [41]. McCluskey said the terms *asynchronous* and *synchronous* were misleading because he had noted that some fundamental mode circuits were directly synchronized by input clock signals (clocked fundamental mode), and that pulse mode circuits could operate with pulse inputs arriving in an asynchronous fashion. He also noted that his definitions did not include all interesting sequential circuits.

More precisely, McCluskey's definitions are as follows. "A sequential circuit is operating in *fundamental mode* if and only if the inputs are never changed unless the circuit is stable internally. A sequential circuit is said to be operating in *pulse mode* if the following conditions are satisfied:

(1) At least one of the inputs is a pulse signal.
(2) Changes in internal state occur in response to the occurence of a pulse at one of the pulse inputs.
(3) Each input causes only one change in internal state" [41, 42].

In defining a pulse, McCluskey made the standard assumptions that a pulse lasts long enough to initiate a change but is gone before the memory elements have changed state. McCluskey, following Cadden [19], demonstrated the different motion of the "operating point" of a flow table depending on whether it was interpreted as a pulse mode or as a fundamental mode flow table. A pulse mode flow table shows only the transitions that take place after the last pulse has gone.

McCluskey objected to the "standard practice" of treating fundamental mode circuits as using feedback loops for storage and pulse mode circuits (possibly due to Caldwell's or Phister's influence, certainly not Mealy's) as using flip-flops. He treated a pulse mode example which had feedback loops [40], he did a fundamental mode example with SR flip-flops [42], and he worked an example of a fundamental mode clocked circuit [40].

McCluskey based his definitions on the basic point that the input sequence to the circuit can be viewed in two ways. If the input sequence has a null or spacer between inputs of interest, then the circuit mode of operation is pulse mode and the behavior can be usefully described by the Moore or Mealy flow table. On the other hand, if each input change is of interest, including those of the clock (if any), and a second condition is met (inputs are not changed until the circuit is stabilized), then the circuit is operating in fundamental mode and a Huffman flow table describes its behavior. We note that McCluskey makes no assumptions about the memory elements or the stray delays (gate delays and line delays) in the circuit. Further, the definition of pulse mode is general enough to encompass both the case where level inputs are gated by a clock pulse (as in Phister) or where all inputs are pulses (as in Caldwell). There is a basic question which fundamental mode operation brings to mind: how does one know when the circuit has stabilized? This question is discussed in Chapter 4.

E. The Differential Mode Model

An edge-sensitive flip-flop responds to either the 0-to-1 or the 1-to-0 transition of a logic signal on an input. These memory elements have appeared in digital systems since at least the early days of discrete transistor logic [43], and they have not always been considered "clocked" or synchronous; yet, very little has been done toward incorporating this useful memory element within the theoretical models and techniques. The work reviewed here is a preliminary step in this direction.

Edge-sensitive flip-flops were mentioned by McCluskey [40]; however, he viewed them as devices for implementing pulse mode circuits. When used in pulse mode circuits, they serve as a direct replacement for pulse-width sensitive flip-flops, and existing analysis and synthesis techniques apply. In this case, special properties of edge-sensitive flip-flops are not used to their advantage. For example, pulse mode techniques do not apply to the counter of Fig. 2.15. The fundamental mode procedures developed by Huffman and extended by others do not directly apply to circuits using edge-sensitive flip-flops. Smith and Roth have studied sequential switching networks that use edge-sensitive flip-flops as the memory elements [44]. These circuits are said to be _differential mode_ (DM) circuits. Smith and Roth note that DM circuits may possess "hidden" transient states. They define the _apparent_ state of a sequential circuit as the state of its inputs and the state of its memory elements. This is not an adequate description of the state for circuits using edge-sensitive flip-flops such as the negative edge-sensitive three-stage binary ripple counter of Fig. 2.15. The operation of the counter is shown by the timing chart. When the input state is the 0-state, and the flip-flops are in the 0-state, the circuit may be in a stable state. However, if the input just went to the 0-state, then the first stage is undergoing a transition to the 1-state. This transient state is "hidden." One cannot faithfully represent a DM circuit by means of a Huffman flow table where each edge-sensitive flip-flop corresponds to a single state variable; the apparent state does not convey enough information. The DM circuit is defined in terms of a 7-tuple $(I, I^*, S, S^*, f, g, z)$. Two new sets, I^* and S^* appear here that do not appear in the customary 5-tuple definition of a finite state automaton. I^* is the set of all ordered pairs of distinct inputs $(I_i, I_j$ where $j = i)$; i.e., it is the set of all input transitions. S^* is the set of all ordered pairs of distinct states; i.e., it is the set of state transitions. The next-state function f is now defined in terms of two forms:

(1) input transitions—if the circuit has reached a stable state; e.g., for stable state S_h, and input change $I_i \rightarrow I_j$, then form $f[S_h(I_i, I_j)]$ applies, or;

(2) state transitions—once an input change has occurred; e.g., for input state I_k and state change $S_i \rightarrow S_j$, then form $f[S_i, S_j), I_k]$ applies.

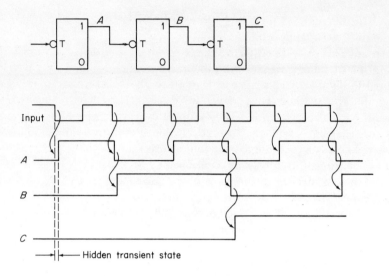

Fig. 2.15. A three-stage binary ripple counter and timing chart.

Although the problem statement of the DM circuit is now amenable to analysis, one can see that the complexity of the description has increased considerably.

Smith and Roth demonstrate that a DM network can model a Moore, Mealy, or fundamental mode circuit. They derive algorithms that convert a fundamental mode (Huffman) flow table to a DM description (7-tuple) and that convert the DM description to a fundamental mode flow table. They define a particularly general I-T (inhibited-toggle) edge-sensitive flip-flop and provide a general synthesis method using this flip-flop as the memory element. Smith and Roth also describe a synthesis procedure for special "ripple" counters. (Figure 2.15 shows a "ripple" counter.) Wareberg and Mergler [45] also describe a method called "subinterval transition mapping." The method uses a flow table to aid the designer's intuition in designing ripple counters that use a single-input, edge-sensitive, toggle flip-flop as the memory element.

F. Flow Table Transformations

An introductory comment by Cadden [19], whose work appeared in 1959, placed it in proper perspective. He noted that the logic designer is usually confined to a certain technology, and that he is generally not interested in making flow table transformations. Thus Cadden did not claim to be developing a tool for the logic designer.

Cadden [19] considered three types of flow tables. Huffman's flow table he called LL for level input and level output. The Mealy flow table was called PP for pulse input and pulse output. (The Mealy table could have many outputs per row, and the output occurred only when the input was present.) The Moore flow table was called PL for pulse input and level output, and for this model, there was only one output per row. For the Mealy and Moore flow tables, the null input N was assumed present when the clock pulse or input pulses were absent. For the Mealy flow table, the symbol N also denotes the null output. The null input, as such, does not exist in the Huffman flow table. Furthermore, it was assumed that no new input changes were made until the circuit was stable. In order to be properly transformable, a Huffman flow table must be in *flow table form* (now called *normal* form); i.e., every unstable flow table entry must lead directly to a stable entry.

In demonstrating a basic difference between the Huffman [10] and Mealy–Moore [2, 22] flow tables, Cadden introduced the important notion of the "operating point." At any given time, the operating point is the present total state in which the circuit is operating. For the Huffman flow table, the operating point moves horizontally in response to the new input column when the input state changes and then moves vertically within the new column to a stable state. The Mealy–Moore flow table does not show the action when the pulse is absent. In order to illustrate the point, Cadden appended a "null" column to the flow table. (Caldwell also did this for expository purposes in relating pulsed sequential circuits to the work of Huffman.) When the pulse is present, the operating point moves horizontally, as in the Huffman case, to the new input column. When the pulse goes away, however, the operating point movement is *diagonally* to the next-state in the null column (see Fig. 2.16).

In going from a Mealy to a Moore flow table, the output associated with the Mealy transition normally would appear right away, i.e., during the presence of the input pulse; but in the equivalent Moore flow table the output appears only after the next-state transition has occurred. Conversely, in going from a Moore flow table to a Mealy flow table, the output appearing at the end of a Moore transition occurs, in the Mealy equivalent, at the start of the transition.

The problems and distinctions are somewhat less trivial in going from the Moore or Mealy tables to a Huffman table than between the Moore and Mealy tables. This is primarily due to the possibility of "like successive inputs." For the case where "like successive inputs" are permitted, Cadden explicitly introduced the null or spacer input N to the Huffman flow table.

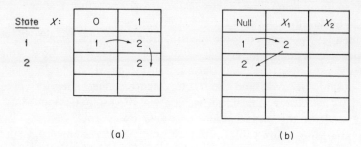

Fig. 2.16. Motion of the operating point. (a) Huffman flow table. (b) Mealy–Moore flow table.

This input is implicit in the Moore or Mealy flow table; the appended "null" column makes it explicit. In going from the Huffman flow table to the Moore or Mealy table, only one output and state transition can occur, i.e., the Moore and Mealy tables are a level of abstraction above the Huffman flow table and cannot represent "cycles." Thus, for the Huffman to Mealy or Huffman to Moore transformations, the Huffman flow table must be in normal form. In formulating the rules for these transformations, Cadden's notion of equivalence is that of Moore [2]; i.e., identical input sequences yield identical output sequences.

G. Minimization Problems

1. The State Reduction Problem

For the completely specified flow table, the Huffman–Mealy–Moore procedure achieves a state reduction solution in a straightforward manner. A convenient tabular method for accomplishing this appears in the work of Gill [46]. For the incompletely specified flow table, Paull and Unger [47] defined an entity called a "maximal compatible" set of states, which is a useful tool in achieving a minimal state flow table. The set of maximal compatibles may be obtained in a straightforward manner. Unfortunately, in the general case there is still no known efficient algorithm (one which does not border on an "exhaustive" search) for solving the problem. Many results apply to subcases of the general problem. An important subcase, where the flow table is incompletely specified only because of forbidden input changes, results in a considerably simplified problem [48]. Mealy [22], Phister [3], Maley and Earle [34] and others have pointed out that minimizing the states or memory elements is not always a good idea; consequently the point is not belabored here.

2. The State-Assignment Problem

The state assignment is the assignment of the particular combinations or codes of the binary state variables to the internal states.

a. Clocked or Pulsed Circuits

If the logic and timing environment precludes the existence of critical races, then the state assignment need not be concerned with eliminating critical races. Under these conditions, the state assignment is usually made to reduce the complexity of the next-state functions by means of a concept called "reduced dependency." The idea here is that if the next state of a particular y variable (one of six, for example) depends on the input variables and only three of the six y variables, then it is probably simpler than a function of all input variables and all six y variables. The partition theory developed by Hartmanis and Stearns [49] provides a tool for solving this problem.

b. Fundamental Mode Circuits

If the circuit delays and timing scheme are not designed to prevent malfunctions through critical races, then the foremost consideration in making a state assignment is to avoid critical races. A solution to this problem is the single-transition time (STT) assignment where all y variables which are to change during a particular transition are excited at once. (The alternative is to require intermediate steps or changes in state before the final state is reached.) Liu [50] introduced the concept of unicode (one code per internal state) STT assignments, and Tracey [51] developed some basic theory associated with these assignments. More recently, the partition theory of Hartmanis and Stearns has been adapted to fundamental mode circuits [52, 53]. A good reference on these considerations is the book by Unger [54].

H. Delays, Hazards, and Constraints on Input Changes

Electrical circuits possess nonzero *stray delays* which appear whenever current or voltage is being switched. The delays due to electrical components of a switching circuit element are called *gate delays*, and delays due to the interconnections are called *interconnection* or *line delays*. For relays, delays result not only from interconnections and the relay coil, but also from contact motion and contact stagger. Stray delays are important because an unfavorable delay distribution might cause undesirable behavior. Much of the work on stray delays and hazards in sequential switching circuits is based on the work by Unger [55].

Since current and voltage are continuous variables, when switched between two values, the signal passes through what Robertson [56] called the "threshold uncertainty region." The threshold uncertainty region gives rise to the phenomenon of different gates connected to the same signal reacting to the voltage or current change at different times. This phenomenon appears as an interconnection delay associated with a gate input. The interconnection delay also depends on the interconnection length, type of adjacent insultation, location of nearby conductors and grounds, the number of gates that share the interconnection, and the state of the gates that share the interconnection. In higher speed circuits, with very fast switching times, the interconnection behaves like a transmission line; consequently, it is subject to reflections and the attendant increased and unpredictable delays unless it complies with the "wiring rules" which constrain interconnection lengths, stub lengths and placement, and require line terminations.

The *gate delay* value is the time between a gate "seeing" an input change that excites it and "responding" with an output change. The stray delay belonging to a memory element is similarly defined. There is also a special device, called a *delay element* or *delay line*, which provides a guaranteed delay value within its tolerance limits. Memory elements sometimes have built-in response times with a guaranteed minimum delay.

The nature of a delay may be pure or inertial. *A pure delay* of value D reflects all input changes on its output at D time units later. An *inertial delay* of D units is similarly defined except a new input value, as a result of a change, must persist for D units before it is reflected at the output. Thus, signal "spikes" or "glitches" (pulses of less than D units duration) are rejected by inertial delays but are passed on by pure delays.

A stray delay constraint is an inequality governing the values the gate or line delays may assume. A *delay assignment* maps each stray delay and instance that the signal changes to a value within the delay constraints. Note that the value of a delay is evident only when a signal changes state and that the delay value may vary from instance to instance. This is due, in part, to variations in ambient temperature, differences between signal rise and fall times, and differences in interconnection delays.

Combinational network hazards, according to Wood's [57] definition, are also known as *static hazards*. When a single input to a combinational circuit changes value and an output signal is to remain "static" (at 0, for example), and it can momentarily change value (to 1) due to stray delays, then the circuit possesses a static hazard. When this occurs in a digital system, it is called a *glitch* or *spike*. By proper combinational network design, this type of hazard may be eliminated.

Wood defines a sequential circuit hazard as a malfunction due to improper circuit timing, where the timing involves stray and feedback delays, and the timing of the input changes. A malfunction is a departure from the predicted or desired signal values that should appear on the signal lines as a result of an input change [13]. If the malfunction creates the wrong stable state, then the malfunction was caused by a steady-state hazard. Here, the *malfunction* is viewed as an actual departure from desired behavior and a *hazard* is viewed as the possibility of a malfunction. The presence of a steady-state hazard in a sequential switching circuit implies the existence of a delay assignment that can cause circuit malfunctions. Thus, the presence of a steady-state hazard is not independent of the delay constraints. Many hazards are due to differences in delays among paths propagating the same signal. Sometimes, in order to avoid hazards, it is necessary to place some constraints on when and how the inputs are allowed to change. In the next section, these assumptions and constraints will be briefly reviewed.

Moore was not particularly concerned with stray delays. He assumed that the memory element state changes took place under the control of a central clock and that the spacing between clock pulses was sufficient to allow the circuit to be settled and ready for each pulse. Mealy assumed that the inputs and outputs were pulses occurring synchronously with the clock as in the technology used in the SEAC.

Huffman [10] dealt mainly with relay circuits. He assumed that the relays provided an inertial delay that was large compared to all the stray delays in the network. He also constrained the input changes to take place only after the network attained a stable condition. More than one input signal could change at a time (multiple-input change), provided they occurred nearly simultaneously (within a given time span).

Unger [14] defined stray delays and treated them as appearing in the gate or in the interconnections. He assumed they behaved as inertial delays and that they had upper bounds. He further assumed the gate delays could be arbitrarily small. He also demonstrated that large pure delay elements (instead of inertial elements) could be used in the feedback loops, provided that there were no race conditions or *combinational circuit hazards* and that only one input was allowed to change at a time [55]. Unger also demonstrated the existence of flow tables that possess essential hazards; these hazards, under his assumptions on stray delays, have no hazardfree realization without the use of delay elements. Flow tables without essential hazards possess delayfree realizations (realizations without delay elements).

Muller, in his work on speed-independent circuits, assumed the stray delays appeared only in the gates, could be arbitrarily large, and were inertial in nature. The interconnection delays were assumed to be zero. He did not permit the use of delay elements. Under these conditions, provided only one input change is made at a time, circuits without steady-state hazards are possible. Since it is assumed that gate delays may be arbitrarily large, then to comply with the constraint that inputs are not changed until the network is stable, the circuit must supply its own completion signal. The proper generation of this completion signal requires considerable ingenuity. A solution based on work of Miller and Winograd is described by Miller [25]; Armstrong *et al.* [58] also provide a solution.

In Maley and Earle [34], delayfree realizations were devised for certain flow tables like the binary trigger which possessed essential hazards. These circuits were called "reliable" because they were "relatively insensitive to malfunctions from the essential hazard." Maley and Earle did not state their delay assumptions, but upon analysis one discovers that they arranged gates so that the essential hazard resulted in a race between a stray line delay and at least one gate delay (with its accompanying line delays). Under the assumption that the single line delay always wins the race, the circuit cannot malfunction and is thus hazardfree. Armstrong *et al.* [15] provided delayfree realization procedures for this delay assumption, while Langdon [16] provided them for similar delay assumptions. Again, the input is constrained to change only one signal line at a time.

Circuits designed using the Huffman flow table may have the "operating point" pass through unstable states. In so doing, a circuit output signal may momentarily change its value. This may occur, for example, between the time the time the circuit "sees" the primary input change, and the secondary variable change. This type of hazard is called a *false output hazard* and may be prevented by properly choosing the output value that is to correspond to the unstable states of the flow table.

Pulsed sequential circuits, such as described by Caldwell [23], require constraints on the input pulse width, otherwise a *pulse-width hazard* may occur: the duration of the pulse must be sufficient to cause memory element toggling, but the pulse must be gone by the time the memory element changes its output values. The memory element has a minimum delay constraint: its output cannot change too soon or a malfunction may result. Memory element outputs are assumed to be levels. The next pulse must not arrive until the circuit resolution time has transpired or a *resolution hazard* results. The *resolution time* is the longest (worst-case) time for an input pulse to propagate through the combinational gating circuit and cause an output change on a memory element. The memory element can be a *JK* flip-flop, SR flip-flop, or delay unit. The input pulses must pass through AND gates (like the gated pulse amplifier in the Whirlwind I) before changing the state of any memory element. In systems where the pulse is not reshaped by the combinational logic gates, then the input pulse cannot cascade through too many gates without experiencing pulse narrowing or broadening.

Wood [57] points out that if the combinational circuit is restricted to two levels (e.g., an AND–OR network), then stray delays are minimized. If it is assured that all AND gates have a pulse input (which means the gate has a pulse output) and all inputs to OR gates are pulses, then a problem occurs only if an OR gate can receive more than one pulse input per state transition. This problem is a *multiple-pulse hazard*. This can always be avoided at the expense of more inputs to AND gates. Caldwell permitted only one input pulse at a time, and Wood [57] has demonstrated the necessity of this condition. Under these conditions no restrictions are placed on the state assignment. If level inputs also exist, they may change state between input pulses (i.e., while the input pulses are in the 0-state). McCluskey has observed that for pulse mode circuit design, the memory elements can be replaced by edge-sensitive (1-to-0) memory elements and the circuit will still work, provided compatibility of the signals and the pulse width exceeds the conditioning time of the flip-flop.

A limiting case of pulse mode operation is where only one pulse input signal exists. This signal may be fed directly to the memory elements; it may also be fed through AND gates (as shown by Phister) or through a special gate to the memory element. This limiting case is often called a single-phase, clocked, sequential network. If a single clock input is explicit and the circuit is allowed to reach a stable state following both clock transitions (1–0 and 0–1), then McCluskey [40] terms the circuit *clocked fundamental mode*. Gray [59] and others point out that in multiphased clock systems (e.g., one with two alternating clock-pulse inputs) the minimum memory element delay constraint disappears provided memory elements that change state on a particular phase do not feed the combinational network that supplies inputs to the memory element of that same phase. This means that the pulse does not need to go away before the memory element changes state; this further implies that level-sensitive memory elements can be used. Wood [57, 60] has studied hazards in pulsed circuits and notes several constraints on delays that disappear when the memory elements clocked at one phase do not feed back to themselves.

Due to stray delays in the combinational network, there is an upper bound on the levels of combinational logic which may be performed. Loomis and McCoy [61, 62] studied this limit although in a different context. Loomis [62] analyzed a system which may be characterized as a two-phase fundamental mode scheme, except the clock phase signals are not precisely spaced. This scheme, the method of analysis, and inequalities he derived is very close to the type of system timing work done by logic designers.

The reason for making assumptions on stray delays and making input change constraints is to avoid the possibility of a malfunction. Broadly

TABLE 2.2.   Design Assumptions and Considerations

Assumptions	Design considerations
(A) Reference: Huffman [10]	
(1) Level inputs, level outputs (2) Multiple input changes (3) Bounded stray delays in combinational network (4) Secondary relays (or feedback loops) have large inertial delay (5) Inputs not changed unless circuit is stable (fundamental mode assumption)	(1) Inertial delays must exceed "hazard time" (2) State assignment must not have critical race
(B) Reference: Unger [55]	
(1) Level inputs, level outputs (2) Single input change only (3) Feedback loops have pure delay elements (4) Bounded stray line and gate delays (5) Fundamental mode	(1) Pure delays exceed the largest cascade of stray delays (2) No critical races between state variables (3) No combinational circuit hazards
(C) Reference: Unger [14, 55]	
(1) Same as B, plus: (2) No essential hazards in flow table	(1) No delay elements needed (2) Special state assignment, implies more than no critical races (3) No combinational circuit hazards
(D) Reference: Muller and Barkey [24], Miller [25]	
(1) Level inputs, level outputs (2) Single-input change[a] (3) Stray line delays are zero (4) Stray gate delays may be arbitrarily large and are inertial (5) No delay elements (implied by 4) (6) No input change unless circuit stable	(1) No critical races between gate output signals (2) Assumption 6 implies a completion signal is required

TABLE 2.2. (Continued)

	Assumptions	Design considerations
(E)	Reference: Armstrong *et al.* [15]	
	(1) Level inputs, level outputs	(1) No critical races
	(2) Single-input change	(2) Special arrangement of the
	(3) No stray line delay exceeds a stray gate delay in value	gates
	(4) No input change until network stable internally	
	(5) Bounded stray delays	
(F)	Reference: Caldwell [23], Wood [57, 60]	
	(1) At least one pulse input, pulse or level outputs	(1) Arbitrary state assignment
	(2) Memory elements provide level outputs	
	(3) Only one pulse input occurs at a time	
	(4) Pulse duration is constrained by a minimum and maximum permissible value	
	(5) Memory element response must exceed a minimum value	
	(6) Level inputs (if any) change between memory element change and next pulse input	

a Implied but not stated.

speaking, malfunctions occur as a result of a signal (either an input or an internal signal) switching too soon or too late with respect to other signals. (In the case of pulse and edge-sensitive memory elements, improper signal rise times or fall times also can cause malfunctions.) The different assumptions and design strategies we have encountered represent different techniques to ensure that signal changes do not occur too soon or too late. To illustrate the variety of approaches, a summary appears in Table 2.2.

I. Classifications

Part of the role of the theorist is to unify, organize, and correlate existing knowledge in his field. We have seen many sequential circuit models which theory has abstracted from the devices and circuits used by the engineers, but very little has been done to classify satisfactorily the models themselves.

The first generation hardware was loosely classified as synchronous or asynchronous. At that time the key feature of the IAS computer's asynchronous operation was the job completion signal. Having classified their models as synchronous, Moore and Mealy termed the Huffman model as asynchronous. At this point, a comment by Richards [63] is in order; he notes that *asynchronous* has been applied to two loosely related but distinct concepts. McCluskey has objected to this ambiguity, and Miller [25] has cautioned against the many different definitions of asynchronous. Hill and Peterson also feel the many uses of the word *synchronous* has rendered it meaningless. In particular, the terms synchronous and asynchronous as applied to the mathematical models are not to be equated with the system timing techniques of the same names found in practical computer systems. Miller [25] also said, "there are many different definitions for 'asynchronous circuit' and 'asynchronous machine' however, and thus one must be careful when encountering these terms."

The confusion began with the two distinct first generation controversies of (1) ac-coupling versus dc-coupling and (2) use of the central clock versus job completion signals for system timing. The two problems were seldom kept distinct. As was stated in 1955 by Kudlich [64] "Two fundamental characteristics of asynchronous computers are vital considerations in the design of such circuits. First, the binary signals in a direct-coupled computer are dc voltage levels rather than trains of pulses produced by a clock. Second, the individual switching operations, such as changing the state of a flip-flop, do not have any predetermined maximum duration. Instead, the machine waits until a signal has been produced, signifying the successful completion of the operation, before initiating the succeeding step."† It can be shown that the assumption that gate or memory element switching delays can be arbitrarily large implies the use of both dc-coupling (rise and fall times cannot be guaranteed) and completion signals.

Alternatively, the term *synchronous* as defined by Mealy, implied both ac-coupling and a central clock, and it was the SEAC machine that Mealy had in mind. From the sampling of first generation computers, we observed that unless one assumes that delays in the gates or memory elements may be arbitrarily large, then there is no need to associate dc-coupling with self-timed systems or ac-coupling with clocked systems. For example, the NAREC computer designers employed capacitive coupling in the actuators

---

† From R. A. Kudlich [64], A Set of Transistor Circuits for Asynchronous Direct-Coupled Computers. *Proc. AFIPS* **7**. © 1955, AFIPS Press, Montvale, New Jersey. Reprinted by permission.

and control circuits, and yet it was a job completion signal that activated the next actuator; conversely, the synchronous IBM 650, except for the timing rings, primarily used dc-coupling. McCluskey's attempt to avoid the ambiguities inherent in the terms *synchronous* and *asynchronous* resulted in the definition of modes of operation called pulse mode and fundamental mode.

In 1966, Gerace observed that the relations between asynchronous and synchronous sequential circuits had not been thoroughly investigated. In his paper [65] he attempted to investigate these relations and to give a unified treatment to electronic sequential circuit realizations.

Gerace defined a pulse input circuit as one that has each input state I_i (where I_i belongs to an input sequence) followed by a null state N. If input I_i causes the circuit to change states to state S_h, then N sets the circuit to S_h. He defined a synchronous mode sequential circuit (S circuit) as one that represents a Mealy or Moore model except that there is apparently no implicit null input. The inputs and the internal state variables change at the same time as in the SEAC. He showed this scheme had transient hazards that could not be eliminated, and apparently forgetting about the implicit "clock-pulse AND," he concluded the model was "impractical" to realize. He proceeded to return the null input to the model, giving it the pulse input property (according to the above definition), and called it a "pulse input synchronous mode sequential circuit" (PS circuit). Time was viewed as a sequence of time increments and during odd time increments an input state I_i was presented; during even time increments the null input N was presented and the internal state change took place. PS circuits were described by a Mealy or Moore flow table with a null input column appended as in Fig. 2.16b.

Gerace defined a normal fundamental mode sequential circuit (F circuit) essentially as McCluskey defined it. Gerace defined a subset of these circuits, "pulse input fundamental mode circuits" (PF circuits) as those F circuits which have the "pulse input" property; i.e., where null inputs separate the input states of the input sequence. These circuits appear to coincide with what McCluskey called "clocked fundamental mode" and what Cadden considered as the result of a transformation to an equivalent Huffman model when "like successive inputs" were permitted. The Huffman flow table has an added "null input" column. The basis for Gerace's "unification" is that since F, S, and PS circuits can be transformed to PF circuits without changing the number of internal states, realizations can now be considered in terms of PF circuits. (But as Cadden pointed out, transformations do little for the logic designer.) He shows how the transformations can take place so that essential hazards and critical race problems are eliminated. Gerarce defines a PFM memory element as the feedback delay model of a binary memory element where both the delayed

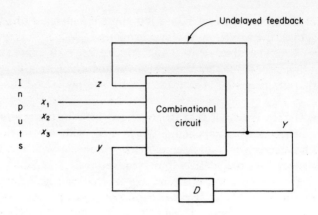

Fig. 2.17.   A PFM memory element.

and undelayed binary signal is fed back to the combinational circuit (see Fig. 2.17).

Besides the works of McCluskey, Cadden, and Gerace, there appears to be little in professional journals dealing with the unification problem addressed by Gerace. However, the various models are often considered in a single framework in books on sequential machines. Wood [57] defined a synchronous circuit as one having the following properties: input changes occur at intervals of delay D; delay elements have values in precise integer multiples of D; there are no stray delays; and all input, output, and internal state variables change state simultaneously. Wood observed that no physical circuit has all these properties, and he proceeded to deal with asynchronous circuits (those circuits for which some synchronous assump-

TABLE 2.3.   Hazards in Sequential Networks

Level sequential	Pulse sequential
Multiple-input change hazard	Pulse-width hazard
Critical race	Multiple-pulse hazard
Resolution hazard	Resolution hazard
Essential hazard	Combinational network hazard
Combinational network hazard	
False-output hazard	
Clocked sequential	
Pulse-width hazard	
Resolution hazard	

tion is violated). In the order of increasing constraints on the inputs, Wood defined sequential networks as: (1) level, (2) pulse, and (3) clocked. These correspond generally to the models studied by Huffman [10], Caldwell [23], and Phister [3], respectively, and they also correspond to the three classifications of Hill and Peterson [11].

Wood illustrated the types of hazards that may occur in these three classifications. The hazards and their decrease with increasing input constraints are shown in Table 2.3.

Unger [54] defined four classes of circuits based upon input constraints, called Huffman, clocked, Muller, and pulse-mode. Huffman circuits constrain the inputs to change only after the circuit has reached some stable situation. Clocked or (synchronous) systems have "an independently generated signal that defines the periods during which input changes are permitted" [54]. In Muller circuits, the input changes are permitted only when the circuit sends an internally generated "ready" signal. For pulse-mode circuits, each input signal line corresponds to an input state, and each input is a pulse, as by Caldwell [23].

J. Sequential Network Interconnections

If the basic timing of a sequential system has a central clock so that the individual memory elements change state under the control of a clock signal, then sequential networks may be interconnected without difficulty. If, on the other hand, the circuits provide pulse outputs and the clock signals are mixed with control signals through gated pulse amplifiers and these pulses are permitted to cascade or chain through many networks (changing the state of memory elements along the way), then the interconnection problem is not straightforward.

Wood [57] comments on the interconnection of sequential networks to form a system. In pulse sequential networks the pulse may cascade through many combinational circuits. Recall that in Whirlwind I the pulse was generated, sent through a distributor network, sent through a decoder network, and then sent to control the data flow. Wood points out that before the system stabilized, a delay of about q times Ds could transpire, where q is the maximum number of cascaded networks and Ds is the worst-case network combinational circuit delay. This can adversely affect the computation rate. On the other hand, a system of clocked sequential networks generally has the computation rate of the single clock source, which is determined by the single combinational circuit delay between two memory elements.

Thus, the Whirlwind I could generally execute more steps of an instruction with a single distributed clock pulse than could be done in one clock time of a single-phase, clocked, synchronous scheme. Further, the Whirlwind I did not need to wait until the entire system stabilized before distributing the next clock pulse; it was only necessary to ensure that the succeeding clock pulse did not "catch up" to its predecessor.

In machines which use job completion signaling, generally only one functional unit is active at a time, and the operations performed by other functional units are inhibited [66]. Control structures that have more than one activity occurring at a time have been studied by Bruno and Altman [67], and many others.

K. A Summary of the Basic Theoretical Developments

Switching circuit theory was stimulated by the use of relay networks in the telephone industry. Boolean algebra was first introduced to describe combinational relay networks, and was subsequently adapted to electronic gate networks. Keister, Ritchie, and Washburn did pioneering work in sequential machine theory, and showed that by using timing charts and operating sequences sequential action could be viewed in intervals, and thus, combinational circuit theory could be applied to the design of the control paths for a sequential network. Montgomerie devised a form of excitation matrix. Reed and Nelson applied Boolean algebra to sequential circuits in the form of flip-flop input equations. (The contributions of these researchers, occurring in 1952 or earlier, go largely unheralded.)

Huffman provided a powerful design tool in the form of a flow table and addressed the state minimization and state assignment problems. His model applied mainly to unclocked networks, but was applicable to clocked schemes as well. Moore, independently using the descriptive tools of the flow table and the transition diagram attacked the state minimization problem. Mealy based his model on the SEAC and slightly generalized the state minimization work of Huffman. Both Huffman and Mealy used the "feedback delay" concept. Muller provided a theoretical basis for the IAS computer philosophy called speed-independent theory. Phister addressed the sequential circuit design process which assumed level inputs and clocked flip-flops, and resulted in a set of flip-flop input equations. Instead of delays in the feedback loops, the model assumes flip-flops; also, single-phase operation of the clock was assumed. We note here that Phister also applied the term "bit-time" to the clock pulse time, a popular term in serial machines. In Chapter 3, Phister's work will be linked to that of the so-called "West-Coast" design tradition. This design method was applied to many early serial machines designed on the West Coast in the 1950's and continues to be popular.

Caldwell addressed pulse mode circuits where the inputs were pulses and only one could change at a time; the memory element outputs were levels. Output pulses and memory element input pulses were provided by combining level and pulse signals in a gated pulse amplifier in a manner reminiscent to the Whirlwind I logic and timing.

Transformations among the Huffman, Mealy, and Moore models were studied by Cadden. Finite automata theorists, interested in behavioral properties, adopted the Moore and Mealy models. McCluskey observed two different basic assumptions on sequential circuit inputs and rules governing how they were permitted to change; he termed them pulse mode and fundamental mode. Although edge-sensitive flip-flops were used in the second generation, only relatively recently has work appeared that treats edge-sensitive flip-flops as memory elements for sequential circuits.

In the course of providing a theoretical basis for various logic and timing philosophies, a large variety of simplification assumptions were made. In particular these concern stray delays, input change restrictions, and memory element operation. Lending a basis and a terminology to these problems, and to constraints due to delays that can arise in circuit operation is perhaps one of the most important contributions sequential switching theory has provided to logic design. (Many logic designers, however, informally understand these problems at the intuitive level.)

Efforts to classify the schemes and models have been attempted. Gerace has sought to unify realization procedures, and Wood has extensively studied and categorized the types of hazards that may occur in the models he studied. This topic is treated again from the logic design viewpoint in Chapter 3.

References

1. S. Seshu, Mathematical models for sequential machines. *IRE Nat. Conv. Rec.* 7, Pt. 2, 4–16 (1959).
2. E. F. Moore, Gedanken experiments on sequential machines. *Automata Studies* (Ann. Math. Studies No. 34). Princeton Univ. Press, Princeton, New Jersey, 1956.
3. M. Phister, "Logical Design of Digital Computers." Wiley, New York, 1958.
4. W. Keister, A. E. Ritchie, and S. H. Washburn, "The Design of Switching Circuits." Van Nostrand-Reinhold, Princeton, New Jersey, 1951.
5. A. D. Friedman, Feedback in asynchronous sequential circuits. *IEEE Trans. Electron. Comput.* EC-15, 740–749 (1966).
6. M. P. Marcus, Relay essential hazards. *IEEE Trans. Electron. Comput.* EC-12, 405–407 (1963).
7. G. A. Montgomerie, Sketch for an algebra of relay and contactor circuits. *Proc. Inst. Elec. Eng. Part 3* 95, 303–312 (1948).
8. I. S. Reed, Symbolic synthesis of digital computers. *Proc. ACM Toronto, Canada Meeting, September 1952*, pp. 90–94.

9. E. C. Nelson, An algebraic theory for use in digital computer design. *IRE Trans. Electron. Comput.* **EC-3**, 12–21 (1954).
10. D. A. Huffman, The synthesis of sequential switching circuits. *In* "Sequential Machines: Selected Papers" (E. F. Moore, ed.), pp. 3–62. Addison-Wesley, Reading, Massachusetts, 1964; first appeared in the *J. Franklin Inst.* **257**, Nos. 3–4 (1954).
11. G. R. Hill and F. J. Peterson, "Introduction to Switching Theory and Logic Design." Wiley, New York, 1968.
12. IBM system/360 I/O interface. IBM Form A22-6843. IBM, 1965.
13. E. B. Eichelberger, Hazard detection in combinational and sequential switching circuits. *IBM J. Res. Develop.* **9** (2), 90–99 (1965).
14. S. H. Unger, Hazards and delays in asynchronous sequential switching circuits. *IRE Trans. Circuit Theory* **CT-6**, 12–25 (1959).
15. D. B. Armstrong, A. D. Friedman, and P. R. Menon, Realization of asynchronous sequential circuits without inserted delay elements. *IEEE Trans. Comput.* **C-17**, 129–134 (1968).
16. G. G. Langdon, Jr., Delay-free asynchronous circuits with constrained line delays. *IEEE Trans. Comput.* **C-18**, 175–181 (1969).
17. G. G. Langdon, Jr., Analysis of asynchronous circuits under different delay assumptions. *IEEE Trans. Comput.* **C-17**, 1131–1143 (1968).
18. M. Krieger, "Basic Switching Circuit Theory." Macmillan, New York, 1967.
19. W. J. Cadden, Equivalent sequential circuits. *IRE Trans. Circuit Theory* **CT-6**, 30–34 (1959).
20. A. L. Leiner, W. A. Notz, J. L. Smith, and A. Weinberger, System design of the SEAC and DYSEAC. *IRE Trans. Electron. Comput.* **EC-3**, 8–23 (1954).
21. J. H. Felker, Typical block diagrams for a transistor digital computer. *Trans. Amer. Inst. Elec. Eng. Part I* **71**, 175–182 (1952).
22. G. H. Mealy, A method for synthesizing sequential circuits. *Bell Syst. Tech. J.* **34**, 1045–1079 (1955).
23. S. H. Caldwell, "Switching Circuits and Logical Design." Wiley, New York, 1958.
24. D. E. Muller and W. S. Bartky, A theory of asynchronous circuits. *Proc. Int. Symp. Theory of Switching, Cambridge, Massachusetts, April 2–5, 1957*. Harvard Univ. Press, Cambridge, Massachusetts, 1959.
25. R. E. Miller "Switching Theory," Vol. 2. Wiley, New York, 1966.
26. R. E. Swartwout, One method for designing speed independent logic for a control. *Proc. Annu. Symp. Switching Circuit Theory and Logical Design, 2nd October 1961*, AIEE Publ. S-134, 94–105.
27. S. C. Kleene, Representation of events in nerve nets and finite automata. *Automata Studies (Ann. Math. Studies No. 34)*, pp. 3–41. Princeton Univ. Press, Princeton, New Jersey, 1956. (From RAND memo RM-704, December 15, 1951 of the same title.)
28. W. S. McCulloch and W. Pitts, A logical calculus of the ideas immanent in nervous activity. *Bull. Math. Biophys.* **5**, 521–531 (1943).
29. M. O. Rabin and D. Scott, Finite automata and their decision problems. *IBM J. Res. Develop.* **3** (2), 114–125 (1959).
30. M. D. Johnson and R. B. Lackey, Sequential machine synthesis using regular expressions. *Comput. Design* **7** (9), 44–47 (1968).
31. T. L. Booth, "Sequential Machines and Automata Theory." Wiley, New York, 1967.
32. J. C. Sims, Jr. and H. J. Gray, Design criteria for autosynchronous circuits. *Proc. AFIPS, Eastern Joint Comput. Conf., Philadelphia, Pennsylvania, December 1958*, **14**, pp. 94–99.

33. J. von Neumann, Probabilistic logics and the synthesis of reliable organisms from unreliable components. *Automata Studies (Ann. Math. Studies No. 34)*, pp. 43–98. Princeton Univ. Press, Princeton, New Jersey, 1956.
34. G. A. Maley and J. Earle, "The Logical Design of Transistor Digital Computers." Prentice-Hall, Englewood Cliffs, New Jersey, 1963.
35. D. E. Muller, Asynchronous logics applied to information processing. *In* "Switching Theory in Space Technology" (H. Aiken and W. F. Main, eds.), pp. 289–298. Stanford Univ. Press, Stanford, California, 1963.
36. D. G. Hammel, Ideas on asynchronous feedback networks. *Proc. Annu. Switching Circuit Theory and Logical Design, 5th, Princeton, New Jersey, October 1964*. IEEE Publ. S-164, pp. 4–11.
37. D. B. Armstrong, A. D. Friedman, and P. R. Menon, Design of asynchronous circuits assuming unbounded gate delays. *IEEE Trans. Comput.* C-18, 1110–1120 (1969).
38. R. K. Richards, "Digital Computer Components and Circuits," Chapters 2 and 3. Van Nostrand-Reinhold, Princeton, New Jersey.
39. M. P. Marcus, "Switching Circuits for Engineers." Prentice-Hall, Englewood Cliffs, New Jersey, 1962.
40. E. J. McCluskey, "Introduction to the Theory of Switching Circuits." McGraw-Hill, New York, 1965.
41. E. J. McCluskey, Fundamental mode and pulse mode sequential circuits. *Inform. Process. Proc. IFIP. Congr. Munich, 1962* (C. M. Popplewell, ed.), pp. 725–730. North-Holland Publ., Amsterdam, 1963.
42. E. J. McCluskey and T. C. Bartee, eds., "A Survey of Switching Circuit Theory." McGraw-Hill, New York, 1962.
43. Transistor component circuits. IBM Form S223-6889. IBM, 1958, 1959. (Available from IBM Branch offices.)
44. J. R. Smith, Jr. and C. H. Roth, Jr., Differential mode analysis and synthesis of sequential switching networks. Clearinghouse Rep. AD-697 189. NTIS, Springfield, Virginia 22151, March 1969.
45. R. G. Wareberg and H. W. Mergler, Designing asynchronous sequential logic circuits. *Contr. Eng.* 14 (10), 99–104 (1968).
46. A. Gill, "Introduction to the Theory of Finite-State Machines." McGraw-Hill, New York, 1962.
47. M. C. Paull and S. H. Unger, Minimizing the number of states in incompletely specified sequential switching functions. *IRE Trans. Electron. Comput.* EC-8, 356–367 (1959).
48. R. J. McCluskey, Minimum-state sequential circuits for a restricted class of incompletely specified flow tables. *Bell Syst. Tech. J.* 4, 1759–1768 (1962).
49. J. Hartmanis and R. E. Stearns, "Algebraic Structure Theory of Sequential Machines." Prentice-Hall, Englewood Cliffs, New Jersey, 1966.
50. C. N. Liu, A state variable assignment method for asynchronous sequential switching circuits. *J. Assoc. Comput. Mach.* 10, 209–216 (1963).
51. J. H. Tracey, Internal state assignments for asynchronous sequential machines. *IEEE Trans. Electron. Comput.* EC-15, 551–560 (1966).
52. C. J. Tan, P. R. Menon, and A. D. Friedman, Structural simplification and decomposition of asynchronous sequential circuits. *IEEE Trans. Comput.* C-18, 830–838 (1969).
53. L. L. Kinney, Decomposition of asynchronous sequential switching circuits. *IEEE Trans. Comput.* C-19, 515–529 (1970).
54. S. H. Unger, "Asynchronous Sequential Switching Circuits." Wiley, New York, 1969.

55. S. H. Unger, A study of asynchronous logical feedback networks. Sc. D. Thesis, Dept. of Elect. Eng., M.I.T., Cambridge, Massachusetts, 1957.
56. J. E. Robertson, Problems in the physical realization of speed independent circuits. *Proc. Annu. Symp. Switching Circuit Theory and Logical Design, 2nd, Detroit, Michigan, October 1961.* AIEE Publ. **S-134**, pp. 106–109.
57. P. E. Wood, Jr., "Switching Theory." McGraw-Hill, New York, 1968.
58. D. B. Armstrong, A. D. Friedman, and P. R. Menon, Design of asynchronous circuits assuming unbounded gate delays. *IEEE Trans. Comput.* **C-18,** 1110–1120 (1969).
59. H. J. Gray, "Digital Computer Engineering." Prentice-Hall, Englewood Cliffs, New Jersey, 1963.
60. P. E. Wood, Jr., Hazards in pulse sequential circuits. *IEEE Trans. Electron. Comput.* **EC-13,** 151–153 (1964).
61. H. H. Loomis, Jr. and M. R. McCoy, A theory of high-speed clocked logic. *Proc. Annu. Symp. Switching Circuit Theory and Logical Design, 6th, Ann Arbor, Michigan, October 1965.* IEEE Publ. **16C13,** pp. 150–161.
62. H. H. Loomis, Jr., A scheme for synchronizing high-speed logic Part II. *IEEE Trans. Comput.* **C-19,** 116–124 (1970).
63. R. K. Richards, "Electronic Digital Systems." Wiley, New York; 1966.
64. R. A. Kudlich, A set of transistor circuits for asynchronous direct-coupled computers. *Proc. AFIPS Western Joint Comput. Conf., Los Angeles, California, March 1955,* **7,** pp. 124–129. AFIPS Press, Montvale, New Jersey, 1955.
65. G. B. Gerace, Sequential circuit realizations with pulse input fundamental mode sequential circuits. *Calcolo* **3,** 493–539 (1966); reviewed by S. Singh, *Comput. Rev.* **9,** 568–569 (1968).
66. W. H. Ware, "Digital Computer Technology and Design," Vol. 2. Wiley, New York, 1963.
67. J. Bruno and S. M. Altman, Asynchronous control networks. *Annu. Symp. Switching and Automata Theory, 10th, 1969.* IEEE Publ. **69C38-C,** pp. 61–73 1969.

Chapter 3

Logic Design Practices

Chapter 1 described logic circuit technologies and timing schemes; Chapter 2 reviewed the models that were derived from these technologies and timing schemes, explained the analysis and synthesis procedures using the models, and attempted to classify the models. In this chapter, logic design is explained relative to the general field of digital system design. The design process based on the symbolic method is explained; associated topics, such as simulation and error detection, are also addressed. System timing, the heart of any digital system, is explained, and logic and timing configurations are classified.

Logic design may mean different things to different people. In this chapter, a broad view is taken. Here, logic design is taken to mean, in addition to "that which logic designers do," topics of interest and concern to logic design such as simulation and test generation.

A. Methods of Design

1. The Design Process

To place logic design in perspective, the phases of a digital system design will be briefly reviewed. A general overview of the design process appears in Table 3.1. At the *architectural level,* one views the system as a black box and is concerned with the appearance of the input and output. At this level, the behavior of the system is described at the operator interface (control panel or console), the programmer interface (instruction set and exceptional conditions), and the input/output interface. At the *systems* (or func-

TABLE 3.1.   Phases of Digital System Design

Architectural		
(1)	Architecture or user	Instruction set
		Input–output (I/O)
		Operator controls
Logic design		
(2)	System or functional design	Checking and maintenance philosophy
		Functional units
		Memory interface
		Registers and data paths (data flow)
		Basic timing cycle
(3)	Symbolic design	Microprogram, register transfers, flow charts
		Auxiliary control and status states
(4)	Detailed logic design	Internal checking
		Maintenance aids, diagnostic program
		Detailed controls and implementation
		Boolean equations, logic block diagrams
		Simulation
Physical design and implementation		
(5)	Physical design	Packaging, card and board layout wiring
		Cable and pin assignment
		Power and cooling
		Documentation
(6)	Check-out	Test
		Debug
		Document updating

tional) *design* level, design objectives and philosophy (such as cost, performance, internal checking, and ease of maintenance) are considered. These considerations affect both the amount and complexity of the major components of a system. In a complex system, the major components might be one or more I/O (input/output) channels, the instruction unit, the execution unit, and the memory bus unit; these components, in turn, might be further decomposed into functional units such as the arithmetic unit, storage data register, accumulator register, counters, decoders, comparators, etc.

Chu [1], among others, has noticed that the logic design level can be broken into three phases. The first phase, called the functional design phase, begins at the lowest functional unit level; it is here where logic design and systems design overlap. In this phase, the *structure*, i.e., the basic registers, arithmetic units, and data paths or data transfer buses, is determined. The result of this phase is generally termed the internal machine organization or *data flow*. Hellerman [2] defines data flow as a diagram showing data paths between different units of the system, but showing neither the generation of control signals nor the control signals themselves. The functional design phase has also been called the "strategic" phase [3]. Another consideration between the functional design phase and the second phase is the system timing, in particular the *machine cycle*. The duration of the machine cycle is the shortest period of time for which data flow events (data transfers, additions, etc.) may repeat themselves. Within one machine cycle there may be many distinct clocking or timing signals. Chu calls the second phase of logic design the *symbolic design* phase. This phase produces a description of *how* the computer performs its functions in terms of the operations or events the data flow is capable of executing. The symbolic phase deals with *behavior*. In the third phase of logic design, called the *detailed logic design* phase, the data flow and its controls are implemented using the technology at hand. The result of this step is generally a set of logic equations.

Because of the strong interaction between functional design and implementation of detailed logic, the functional design itself might change. For example, one might want to shift an adder input to assist the multiply and divide operations. Also, one might decide that a particular data flow register could be avoided by providing an additional data path to another register. There are a few problems that, although they should be addressed earlier, are sometimes left to the detailed design phase; these include problems with internal checking, information paths to and from the operator console, and hardware to assist in maintenance and checkout.

The next step in the design process is the physical *packaging* of the logic. This phase is very dependent on the technology. Typically it involves assigning logic gates to modules, modules to cards, cards to boards; making pin assignments; routing wires; placing cards on the boards; and making cable socket assignments. Note again that with circuit speeds and circuit densities increasing by an order of magnitude and connector pins remaining about the same size, the packaging phase is today becoming the most critical phase of the design of many computers.

After packaging, and a machine is built, the design is checked and debugged. Note that there is no clear definition between each phase; e.g., in smaller systems the architecture and system design phases may be the same phase (called functional design). For small digital controllers, the logic design phase might consist only of the functional design and the detailed logic design phase. Also, there is usually considerable overlap between the detailed logic design phase and the check-out phase. A general description of the design process also appears in the paper by Moon [4].

The general field of digital system engineering, although it includes logic and system design, has a wider meaning. The term must also include the endeavors of those who engineer the power system; the cooling system; the mechanical design of the frames, gates, boards, and cards; the cabling; and the wiring. It includes the activities of those working on the design automation and the documentation systems. Digital system engineering also comprises testing, diagnostic and checking procedures, simulation, microprogramming, and maintenance. Further, the architecture of a computer system (and/or its design) may be strongly influenced by the work of those who analyze, simulate, measure, or evaluate the performance or behavior of digital systems. Thus, a considerable diversity of practical problems exists in digital system engineering, and logic design is only a small, but nevertheless important, part of the whole.

2. The Logic Designer

The job of the logic designer (sometimes called "logician") is to realize or implement the functional units and their interfaces with the available technology. Hellerman described the job as follows: "The logic designer is typically presented with a specification of a logical function and a maximum time delay for the circuit which is to implement this function. He is also usually restricted to using specified logic blocks with their fan-in,† fan-out,‡ and time-delay constraints" [2]. For example, the IBM System/360 Model 50 computer used SLT (Solid Logic Technology). The result of a logic implementation is often represented by a set of wiring diagrams showing how the decision and memory elements are interconnected. In general, the logic designer initially works with the systems designers because he may determine certain desirable changes in the functional organization that may more readily or economically provide the desired external features for the computer [5]. Bensky [6] speaks of the creative aspects of logic design. Creative efforts require the ability to visualize and comprehend, both in space and time, the following: the data flow and control information, the relation of these to the timing within and between the computer's units, and the factors of interdependence.

3. The Eastern and Western Schools

One of the topics at the 1958 Western Joint Computer Conference was how to best implement the logic of a machine. Two schools of thought emerged—the Eastern and the Western. The Eastern school emphasized the

---

† Maximum number of input signals to a gate.
‡ Maximum number of gates loading a single signal line.

use of block diagrams and the Western school emphasized the use of Boolean equations in implementing a design.

The Eastern school of logic design is the oldest. It makes use of block diagrams or logic diagrams in laying out a section of logic. A block diagram shows the logic blocks or gates and their interconnections for a section of logic. Basically it shows signal names and the type of gate; but it may also be used to display physical packaging information such as signal pin locations. In defending the Eastern school, Bensky [6] emphasized the necessity to visualize the system, its data transfer paths, registers, and basic timing, and pointed out that block diagrams afford rapid comprehension of these items. He felt that creative improvements could be made to a design with this visualization.

Richards [7] states that there is some use of Boolean algebra or logic equations in the design process, but that one cannot rely exclusively on them. The logical equation approach works best when the computer is viewed as a large number of bistable memory elements and time is divided into discrete steps, where the state of the bistable elements at each step is a function of their state at the end of the previous step. But not all portions of a computer work this way (e.g., the ripple-carry counter or a trigger accumulator). Also, not all systems lend themselves to logical equation characterization (e.g., a system where two or more pulses may follow each other along a chain of cascaded gated pulse amplifiers). Richards makes the point that manufacturing and maintenance personnel find block diagrams more understandable and that the diagrams conveniently afford a correlation between logical functions and physical locations of blocks and pins.

As a proponent for the Western school, Engel [8] pointed out that logical equations are readily entered into a computer, and that in this form three convenient operations may be performed. First, statistics such as fan-out and "gate counts" may be obtained. Second, a wiring list may be drawn. And third, the computer under design may be simulated, which reduces the cost of check-out. In citing advantages for the Western school, Hesse [3] noted that logical equations are adaptable to formal minimization procedures and may result in a more economical design. He also observed that Boolean equations are more compact than block diagrams. Hesse divided logical design into two phases: the "strategic," which determines the overall data paths and configuration, and the "tactical," which primarily determines the final form.

In the open discussion session at the 1958 Western Joint Computer Conference, the point was made that East-Coast computers tended to be parallel in nature and West-Coast computers were serial in nature. Richards commented that the relative merits of logic equations seemed machine dependent, the simpler "serial-binary" computers lending themselves more easily to logic equations. Another point brought out by debaters at the conference during the open discussion was that in diode logic the operations performed are the Boolean AND and OR, whereas the situation becomes more complicated in NAND or NOR transistor logic. NOR and NAND circuits are more difficult to apply, both for logic equations and block diagrams.

Perhaps the resolution to the East–West controversy on logic design is seen in a report by Cole and Zimmerman [9]. The report described a digital system and made extensive use of timing charts and block diagrams to show overall functional unit layout and to demonstrate particular circuit implementations such as a comparator and module switch. However, in the Western tradition, Boolean equations were used to describe compactly the input equations of flip-flops used for control.

4. Symbolic Methods

As previously mentioned, the logic design process consists of three phases: the functional-design phase, the symbolic method (or symbolic-design phase), and the detailed logic-design phase. In the *symbolic method,* the structure has been defined and the problem is to express the execution of the machine instructions as a sequence of symbolic statements. In 1957, Frankel [10] described the major logic design structure of the LGP-30, a first-generation drum computer, in this manner. The LGP-30 computer's data flow essentially consisted of three circulating registers on three drum tracks. In addition, 15 control and track selection flip-flops were used.

A more sophisticated symbolic technique was employed in describing the CG24, a computer similar to the IBM 704 built by the MIT Lincoln Laboratory [11]. Dinneen *et al.* introduced a "register transfer language" and used it to describe their design. The statements generally had arrows to demonstrate the flow of information and the operations performed as the data were moved. Each statement corresponded to a data flow *event* or *micro-operation.* Included in the statement was timing information, the state of the phase or control counter, and whether the machine was in the instruction fetch state or the instruction execution state. A conditional operator could be appended to the statement; if the operator were false, the micro-operation would not occur.

Dinneen's paper is of interest because it describes a technique of the second logic design phase (the symbolic phase) which in one form or another is currently used: the specification of *control states,* and the one or more data flow events (or micro-operations, or register transfers) that each control state accomplishes. To execute a machine instruction, the computer passes through some sequence of the control states.

In their notation, fi is a control signal which, when in the 1-state, means the current *control state* is *i*. The statement

$$fi: \quad (A) \rightarrow B, (C) \rightarrow D$$

means that during control state *i*, the contents of register A are transferred to register B, and the contents of register C are transferred to register D.

In the CG24, a control state corresponded to one 12-microsecond memory cycle. The memory cycle, which is also the machine cycle, was further subdivided into four substates, *P1*, *P2*, *P3*, and *P4*. The instruction fetch cycle was denoted af2. Here, "a" means instruction fetch, a' was used to denote instruction execution cycles.

To illustrate the notation, the instruction fetch cycle is described. The portion of the data flow of interest is a memory M, its address register MAR, its data register MDR, and a register D which may be counted up. During instruction fetch, the following occur:

$|af\,2P1\,|$: $(M\langle MAR\rangle) \rightarrow MDR, (MAR) \rightarrow D$

$|af\,2P2\,|$: $(MDR) \rightarrow M\langle MAR\rangle, (I[MDR]) \rightarrow$ Control Unit

$|af\,2P3\,|$: $(D) + 1 \rightarrow D$

$|af\,2P4\,|$: $(Ad[MDR]) \rightarrow MAR$

In the above cycles, during *P1*, the content of the memory M location specified by MAR is read out to MDR, and also the content of MAR is copied into D. During *P2*, the content of the MDR is rewritten into the memory word from which it was read since the reading of a core memory location destroys its contents. Also in *P2*, the instruction code portion (I[MDR]) of the instruction (now found in MDR) is transferred to the control unit. The instruction code will subsequently be used to specify the sequence of control states required for its execution. At *P3*, counter D is increased by one. (At the end of instruction execution, D can be transferred to MAR in preparation for fetching of the next instruction.) At *P4*, the address portion of MDR is transferred to the MAR, in preparation for operand fetch.

These basic steps form a part of the instruction fetch portion of most contemporary computers, and although the method a logic designer uses to specify the steps may vary, some sort of notation (be it a flow chart, timing chart, or a tabular version of the symbolic notation) is required.

The idea of using arrows and register transfers in describing this phase of a machine's logic design apparently occurred to many designers; for example, Glaser [12], and Hudson *et al.* [13] used this technique. A variation used by these designers [12, 13] is the flow chart, used extensively by programmers. It can be used in logic design to show the sequential relationship and branching operations between symbolic statements. The data flow events or micro-operations that occur in the same machine cycle are placed in the same flow chart block, and lines connecting possible successor flow chart blocks are indicated on the diagram.

The result achieved during the *symbolic design* phase is the same accomplishment achieved by microprogramming: the list of micro-operations required to execute all the instructions in the instruction set of the computer [14]. Thus, the result of this second phase is a "microprogram" that fetches, decodes, and executes the machine language instructions. Wilkes, who was the first to use the term microprogramming, regarded microprogramming as an orderly means of designing the control unit of a digital computer with a fixed instruction set [15]. He viewed microprogramming as an alternative to the ad hoc conventional methods of design.

Many means exist for storing and accessing microprograms; most often due to cost considerations, some sort of a read-only store is employed (usually called a control store). Some interesting means of accessing microprograms can be seen by examining the MIT CG24, the Burroughs 220, and the NCR 304 computers. The MIT CG24 used a diode matrix, addressed from a data-flow register named G. The word read from the matrix was placed in the F register. The F register outputs controlled gates for register transfers for the machine cycle and provided for a next address to be placed in register G. Concerning the Burroughs 220, Glaser [12] speaks of microprogramming but makes no mention of a read-only store; rather, he speaks of converting the flow charts to circuit and wire lists. The control store of the NCR 304 is implemented by a specially wound core matrix [13].

The condition necessary for the success of the symbolic method is discussed by Eachus in describing the Honeywell H-290 computer: that there be a clearly defined controlled section, or data flow. This way, any changes in the instruction set will not affect the wiring and content of the controlled section [16]. In conjunction with the design of the controlled section, which was a general-purpose data flow, a set of control signals for that data flow was listed. The control signals, when activated, performed micro-operations such as transferring data, controlling the adder, setting or clearing flip-flops, or controlling the memory or input/output equipment.

Thus, the essential ingredient of a systematic approach to the symbolic design phase is a well-defined structure (data flow or "controlled section"). The controls express behavior and may be described by flow charts, or in a register transfer language, or by a microprogram. They may be implemented through conventional circuits (called hard-wired logic) or with a control store of switch cores, diode matrices, or any other suitable means (now called control memory). A general description of this design phase using symbolic notation is presented by Chu [1] and Bartee *et al.* [17, Chapter 9]. Introductory descriptions of microprogramming appear in Vandling and Waldecker [18] and Rosin [19].

5. Flow Chart Procedures

Flow charting techniques [20] have been applied to computer programming since the birth of the electronic computer [21]. It is natural to apply these techniques to logic design [12, 13]. The arithmetic controls for the Illiac II computer were described using flow charts [22, 23]. First, the functions of the arithmetic unit, independent of its controls, were defined. Then, in the symbolic phase of logic design, the controls were described. The control signals consisted primarily of register gating signals, selector signals for governing the information source for data entered into registers, and control signals to set or clear status flip-flops. The flow chart provided the ordering in time of the micro-operations necessary to execute a given instruction, or subsequence of an instruction [22]. The notation used in these charts appears in the work of Gillies [24] and also of Miller [25].

Gorn *et al.* [26] advocate the use of flow charts to describe the execution of a machine's instruction set. They describe a process for converting a tabular or logical equation format to a flow chart. Here the flow chart, used during the design phase, would provide a basis for simulation on another machine and later could provide the machine language programmer with a better understanding of the behavior of the machine.

In 1962 Rutherford [27] advocated techniques for the use of flow charts in digital system design. The method was used in the construction of two digital systems. At the internal machine organization level, the data flow throughout the system is shown on system block diagrams. A system flow chart and a basic system-timing chart is also built. The system flow diagram is a flow chart describing all contingencies for system operation.

> The extent to which the flow diagram will be detailed will vary from system to system, but, in general, its symbols will contain questions and statements specifying what operation is to be performed rather than *how* it is performed. For example, if the "Enter Data" key is down, then read data from the "Card Reader" into storage [27].

Blocks are two shapes, diamond and rectangular. Information within diamond blocks asks a question (e.g., "Enter Data Key down?"). Information within rectangular blocks states operations or output signals (e.g., "Read Card Data to Storage"). An example of a portion of a system flow diagram taken from Rutherford [27] is shown in Fig. 3.1. Timing at this stage of design is a sequence chart; the time is the abscissa which shows

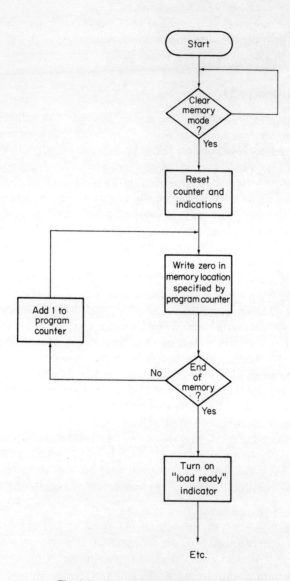

Fig. 3.1. Example of system flow chart.

the period of existence and timing dependencies for each control and data path.

It is necessary to provide more detail to the system flow diagram to show how operations are accomplished. For example, an operation block stating "Calculate Parity" for a serial-by-bit input line may be expanded into several blocks concerned with the setting and clearing of two flip-flops. In addition, timing information must be provided; this may take the form of the insertion of decision blocks labeled "T4 Time?". When the flow diagram has been reduced to conditions that provide output signals or which set or reset flip-flops, then the flip-flop input equations can be obtained. Some of the special-purpose status flip-flops can be eliminated by "time-sharing" with other status flip-flops; i.e., two flip-flops that are used during different, mutually exclusive operations can be "merged." This merging process replaces many special-purpose status flip-flops with a few, general-purpose status flip-flops.

MacKinnon also favors the flow chart method and has designed several systems using the approach. The flow chart is refined to the point of interconnecting Boolean equations [28]. In the example MacKinnon worked out, greater detail was added to the original flow chart, such as determining where status flip-flops were needed in order to tell which paths had been followed. At the final flow chart step, the operation blocks with statements such as "Set FFA" are replaced by Boolean equations such as "Set FFA = A(CTR5) + B(CTR12)." Flow charts are also used extensively by Chu in his book [29] to describe sequences of micro-operations.

Note that the detailed flow charts convey the same information as a state transition graph. One detects an input change in the decision (diamond) blocks, and outputs (and internal state changes) occur in operation (rectangular) blocks. Thus in addition to describing a sequential switching circuit by means of a state transition graph, a flow table, a 5-tuple, or by a regular expression, the flow chart may also be used. In fact, this is a practical descriptive method and appears in many machine descriptions and manuals.

Unfortunately, formal procedures for treating flow charts do not exist, but Hartson [30] describes a flow chart oriented language called DCSL (Digital Control Simulation Language) for simulating a digital control system. Since the problem is primarily intended for digital systems that are described by flow charts, conversion from a flow chart to DCSL is quite convenient. In fact, Moon [4] proposes that the result of the symbolic design phase be converted to a functional flow chart, which he calls a state-operation diagram. This diagram becomes the basic reference for functional simulation.

6. Logic Design Languages

After the development of symbolic notation, the next evolutionary step in describing logic was the development of formal languages. The formal language, used as input to a computer program, may convert the description of the digital system logic into Boolean equations and may also provide a basis for simulating the system. As systems are designed by an iterative process, design changes may be handled by changing the computer input.

In 1962 Gorman and Anderson [31] designed a system description language (SDL) in conjunction with their Logic Design Translator (LDT) system. LDT is a programming system that produces Boolean equations of an entire system. Sequences of micro-operations are described by statements in this language. Declarations are used to specify the system structure or data flow (i.e., the registers, equipment such as arithmetic units, and permissible data paths or buses). Greater detail on the LDT system, including the use of a timing program and its application to an actual design, is given by Proctor [32]. The language, SDL, is strongly influenced by the structure of ALGOL, a high-level programming language. More recently, Gorman reports the development of an expanded systems design language called SDL II for describing both hardware and software of a digital system [33].

Another language suitable for describing both the hardware and software of a system, but unique in many other respects, was developed by Iverson [34, 35]. Iverson's language or notation (APL),† is a very powerful general-purpose language, finding applications in microprogramming, switching theory, operations research, and information retrieval. The language systematically extends a set of basic operations to vectors and matrices, and possesses a family of flexible "selection" operations. Hellerman uses this notation extensively in his book on digital systems [2]. Several digital systems have been described in Iverson notation, including the IBM System/360 [36]. This latter achievement was termed an "important milestone" by Bell and Newell [37]. Friedman and Yang [38] have developed a computer program called ALERT which converts a machine description in Iverson notation to Boolean equations; this program has been applied to the IBM 1800 computer. As with previous efforts, the description of the data flow or controlled section was handled by declaration statements.

Chu has developed an ALGOL-like computer design language called CDL [39]. The language can describe computer elements (functional units such as registers, decoders); can express timing signals and register

† A Programming Language.

transfers; and can precisely specify micro-operations and their sequencing. The design at this level is termed the "macro logic design." McCurdy and Chu [40] have developed for CDL a translator which converts the macro logic design into a set of Boolean equations.

Several other formal languages for describing computers have been developed; these include Schorr's Register Transfer Language [41], Schlaeppi's LOTIS (logic, timing, and sequencing) language [42], a FORTRAN-like language by Metze and Seshu [43], DDL by Duley and Dietmeyer [44, 45], and ISP (Instruction Set Processor) by Bell and Newell [37].

An aspect of computer system description and simulation which should be addressed is the existence of concurrent activity in the system. This does not mean that an operation block of a flow chart will contain more than one action; rather it does mean that the system may be most usefully viewed as consisting of more than one flow chart. This point was considered in the formal description of System/360, where a "dwell" operator had to be appended to the Iverson notation to handle the fourteen kinds of concurrent operations [36]. Examples of concurrent operations are the CPU, the timer, the control panel, interrupts, and each I/O channel. For the ALERT project, Friedman and Yang also viewed a computer description as consisting of a set of distinct descriptive microprograms in modified Iverson notation; each microprogram had its individual timing so that it could execute concurrently with the other microprograms. Along these same lines, Hartson [30] defines "External Dependent" signals. These signals, such as "STOP," are important to the system, but they would cause excessive clutter if included on every diamond block of the system flow chart.

7. Logic Simulation

To the logic designer, simulation means that he must supply to a computer program the description of his system and a sequence of primary inputs. The simulator program will exercise the system based upon the sequences of primary inputs and will provide the logic designer with the sequence of outputs or internal signal states. The purpose of the simulation will generally dictate the form of the simulator program. The most common purpose for simulating is to check out and debug the design, sometimes called *design verification*. Design verification can take place at two levels, corresponding to the two levels of logic design, symbolic design and detailed design. A second purpose of doing design verification is to assist in devising acceptance tests for printed-circuit cards once logic has been placed on them, the simulation a designer applied to verify his design ought also to test it. Another objective for simulation is to determine the symptoms of faults in the computer, called *fault simulation*. Fault simulation is done at the gate level or detailed design level, and it takes place on a "bad" machine (a "good machine" with a fault injected). A fault might be a gate output stuck-at-1 (s-a-1) or stuck-at-0 (s-a-0). Fault simulation is used in several ways. At the system level, a dictionary of "symptoms" where certain faults cause a deviation from "good machine" behavior is compiled to assist maintenance personnel in locating the fault within a machine. Fault simulation is also used to test the effectiveness of sets of tests, or diagnostic or internal checking programs. At packaging levels such as the printed circuit card, fault simulation can be used to check the "coverage" of card tests and in addition to simple failure detection, help pinpoint the faulty component. This latter feature is called *diagnosis*. Thus design verification places emphasis on whether or not the system works as designed, and fault simulation assists in diagnosing where the system or unit failed so the faulty part can be replaced.

Design verification at the register transfer level may be used to check the data flow events or micro-operations designed during the symbolic design phase. A discussion of this problem and the description of a language to do this appears in the book by Chu [29, Chapter 5]. At this level, simulation can be relatively fast because the detail of how the micro-operations are carried out at the gate level is avoided.

When performing design verification at the gate or logic element level, a consideration arises which is called the figure of merit by Breuer [46] and the "slowdown ratio" (SDR) by McKay [47]. The SDR may be viewed as the ratio of time to simulate a machine performing some function versus the actual time for the machine itself to perform it. Thus, if a simulated machine is designed to execute a particular instruction in 2 microseconds and if it takes the simulator program about 200 milliseconds of computer time to simulate the instruction, the SDR is 100,000:1.

A review of reasons for doing simulation for design verification at the gate level is presented by Lake [48]. The design verification application appears to be the first use of simulation in logic design [8].

There are two major approaches to simulation at the gate level, called the *compiler* and the *interpreter* techniques respectively. In the compiler approach, each gate is represented by a Boolean equation. Upon assignment of values 1 or 0 to the primary inputs and flip-flops (the "level 0" functions); the gate outputs of gates at "level 1" (gates whose inputs come from only level 0 signals) can be calculated from evaluating the Boolean equation. Gates at level i receive inputs from level $i - 1$ or less. In the analysis phase, these equations are ordered according to level, then the compiler produces a program whose execution determines each gate's new output by evaluating its Boolean equation at the proper time. In the compiler approach, the structure of the simulated system is absorbed into the compiled program. The analysis phase is necessary because it orders these equations into levels such that the outputs of gates at levels needed for evaluation at the next level have already been calculated. This is convenient for machines where the only feedback occurs within flip-flops and the flip-flops are all clocked. Some level 0 functions, i.e., the flip-flop next-state functions, are actually evaluated last. The compiler approach was used by Seshu and Freeman [49].

An alternative to the compiler approach is the interpretive approach. For this approach, the machine representation generally consists of a set of subroutines for evaluating the functional or logic blocks, plus a list defining how the blocks are interconnected. For each block type, the subroutine will go to a table to obtain the proper input values and will evaluate the outputs of the block. If the block output changed, then blocks fed by the changed block are placed on a list to be evaluated. In the interpretive approach, the structure of the simulated system appears in the lists or tables operated on by the simulator program. This type of simulator is also called a table-driven simulator.

In evaluating the output of a block. Breuer states the method can be data-dependent or data independent [50]. Data-dependent evaluation generally has computer instructions that branch on values, whereas data-independent evaluation uses the computer's Boolean (AND, OR) and complementation instructions. The latter method is important for fault-simulation considerations as can be seen from the following example. If a 36-bit word is used to represent the binary values for a particular logic element output under 36 different fault conditions, and the evaluation procedure operates on the 36-bit words in a data-independent routine, then 36 faulty machines can be simulated at once, affording a potential 36:1 reduction in the slowdown ratio.

It has been noted that only a portion of a machine's logic is active during any simulation pass and the SDR can be improved by calculating values only for the "active" blocks. If no input to a block changes, its output need not be recalculated. This feature was incorporated in the SLDA simulator [51]. This approach also was mentioned by Breuer [50] and has been pursued by Ulrich [52, 53].

The problem of simulating stray delays has been handled in many ways. For simulators of clocked systems where every gate receives a clock signal, stray delays present no special problem [54]. If this is not the case, then the design verification process should include some hazard analysis. Shalla provides a method of analyzing critical races or oscillations [55]. This method essentially traces out an "allowed sequence graph" for simultaneously changing signals to verify that all possible orders of changes result in the same stable state. This work is thus based on the assumption that interconnection delays are zero. The simulator described by Shalla provides for only 47 blocks having stray delay, and thus it is not practical for large systems.

Another method to handle stray delays is described by Eichelberger [56] and implemented in a system called 3V SIM, described by Jephson *et al.* [57]. Many systems use the value 0 or 1 to denote the value of a logic element output; however, the three-value system uses, in addition to these, the value X to denote a signal which is either "unknown" (such as for initializing) or in a state of change (changing 1-to-0 or 0-to-1). The truth tables for two-valued logic blocks are readily converted to three-valued truth tables [56]. Data-independent routines are used, and evaluation takes place in two passes. For the first pass, the X pass, all changing primary inputs are first changed to X, and any active blocks are evaluated. For the second pass, the V pass, the changing primary inputs are now given their new value (0 or 1), and any active blocks are again evaluated. Input changes presented to delay elements cause additional "delayed" X pass and V pass pairs. Langdon [58] has studied the delay assumptions under which this analysis holds, and they coincide with those of Unger [59]. That is, stray delays are assumed to consist of both line and gate delays, and a line delay can exceed a chain of gate delays. Thus the Eichelberger method will turn up "essential" hazards in binary triggers constructed from gates. This delay assumption is, therefore, a source of complaints from logic designers because it requires "dummy" delay blocks to be inserted in the logic. Another disadvantage of the Eichelberger method is that it will not check the worst-case delay paths. It is advantageous because it easily handles feedback loops and because it is fast. At the end of the final delayed V pass, it is ready for the next primary input change.

To correct the pessimistic delay assumptions of 3V SIM, Tung [60] devised a "unit delay" algorithm in 1965. The algorithm is suitable for either two-valued or three-valued simulators. Essentially it assigns a unit of delay to each gate and thus avoids the essential hazard problem, but it also provides less chance of detecting a legitimate critical race.

Smith also attacks the problem of stray delays, but he uses a simulator clock [61]. Here, each block is assigned a minimum delay value TD and an ambiguity value TA. The ambiguity value TA represents the "spread" of the stray delay. The "best-case" delay value is thus TD and the "worst-case" delay value is the sum of TD and TA. For each logic element, Smith keeps three bits of information: the "old value," the "new value," and a "hazard value"; thus a signal line may take on one of eight values. With this information he can realistically simulate the "spread" of a signal as it propagates through a chain of gates. He uses a simulator clock and orders of events in the proper time sequence. Lists are kept of blocks which are fed by each block, as well as events which may be set off by a 1–0 or 0–1 transition (as in the case of edge-sensitive flip-flops). A brief history of edge-sensitive flip-flop input changes is also kept so that a short pulse (spike) or near simultaneous conflicting inputs can be flagged. It is interesting that, in addition to the "realistic" simulator version, Smith proposes an "idealized" version. In the idealized version, delay spreads are ignored and logic hazards are not detected, but the overall behavior may be simulated at a more favorable slow down ratio.

The work by Ulrich [53] also presents a scheme where time is explicitly accounted for. A list of time slots is maintained; each time slot represents possible times at which future events may occur. These time slots are either null or point to a sublist of events. As present actions cause future events, they are placed on the proper sublist. Here, logic element delays are given a particular value (no "spread" is assumed), and signal values may be either 1 or 0. In extending the basic method, Ulrich mentions that block 1–0 transitions may be given a value different from the 0–1 transition, and that possibly a random number generator could be used to assign delay values within a "spread."

When considering fault simulation for a complex system, the possible number of failures that could be simulated becomes quite large, and methods that reduce the SDR take on increased importance. Under these conditions, it is sensible to use data-independent evaluations so that many machines can be simulated at one time. To further reduce the SDR, the simulator is generally not written in some high-level programming language. The detection of hazards and critical races, important for design verification, takes on secondary importance. Techniques such as simulating only logic elements whose inputs change are also incorporated to reduce the SDR. Manning and Chang [62] describe several fault simulation techniques; more recently they suggest that one simulate only the failed functional unit at the detailed level and that time may be saved by simulating the other functional units at a higher or behavioral level (e.g., use table look-up for a sequential circuit) [63].

Logic simulation, in summary, is performed on digital logic for more than one reason. The form in which the machine is described for documentation purposes (Boolean equations or logic elements and interconnection list) may influence the form of the simulator. The purpose of doing a particular simulation may determine the level of detail simulated and the philosophy in handling critical races or hazards.

8. Control of Malfunctions and Failures

The early literature indicates a strong interest in methods of checking the computer. When the computer was a new tool, vacuum tube failures were common; thus the users, generally mathematicians, needed some assurance that the results of the computer were correct. In the ENIAC, the *checking strategy* consisted of several techniques. A ten-minute program that exercised all units of the system was run at the beginning of each day, and every hour the operator was supposed to run a two minute check routine that exercised the most frequently used units. Another technique included running each problem twice and comparing the results. Eckert estimated that this introspective checking strategy, when followed, consumed about 60% of the available machine time [64], but that the operators often omitted it. As a result, this checking and diagnostic strategy proved uneconomical in practice.

Two general classes of checking exist, low-level checking and high-level checking [65]. Examples of low-level checking are (1) the use of the bi-quinary code in the early Bell Computers and (2) the popular odd–even or parity check, where an additional bit is attached to each word in memory. High-level checking is generally the responsibility of the computer user. This method was used on the ENIAC, where checks were made on solutions to problems. Other examples of high-level checking are solving a problem in two-ways, using reasonability tests on answers, and computing something known and comparing against the known result.

Today, low-level checking is called "internal checking" or "built-in checking." An early example of a computer designed with the built-in checking philosophy was BINAC, a computer system whose design called for duplication [65]. In the UNIVAC I, internal functional units (such as the adder, major data flow registers, and counters) were duplicated, and their two outputs were compared [66, 67]. In addition, parity bits were used to check UNIVAC I data transfer paths and memory; consequently, about 30% of the UNIVAC I circuits were for checking. Eckert felt that this type of built-in checking was the best approach to error control. Eckert's experience dictated that the faith one could put in the answers provided by an unchecked machine was "exceedingly low" [67].

Buchholz expresses a different checking philosophy when describing the IBM 701 computer. He observed that there was not complete agreement at that time as to how to check scientific calculations properly, that the value of built-in checking was doubtful, and thus the IBM 701 had very little of it [68]. The computer application often determines the extent of checking. For example, the IBM 650 computer, intended for commercial data processing, used weighted codes and validity checks to check internally data paths, the memory, and the arithmetic unit. On the other hand, some present-day manned aircraft computers have no built-in checking other than a parity bit in memory; high level checking is provided by a special checking program which runs periodically [69]. If a failure is discovered, the pilot simply turns off the computer.

The logic designer may use many techniques for internal checking. Arithmetic codes exist for checking addition; however, techniques also exist for checking addition using a parity check [70]. In addition, duplication of units has also been used. Some work has been done in designing counters that incorporate a validity check. A general approach to checking circuits appears in Carter and Schneider [71].

In order to control faults in a digital system, some redundancy is included in the system. The additional logic circuits either (1) "tolerate" (or "mask") the effect of a faulty component or (2) assist in testing and diagnosing. Von Neumann sparked early interest in *fault-masking* or *protective redundancy* techniques [72]. Out of this work came the *triple modular redundancy* (TMR) approach to fault masking, which was employed in the computer of the Saturn V launch vehicle [73, 74]. The Saturn computer was divided into seven functional units; each unit was subdivided into replaceable modules. Seventeen replaceable modules were triplicated, and the outputs were determined by majority gates.

Another approach to "masking" detected faults is to retry the operation that effected the failure. This approach was used on the Bell Computer Model VI, and was called the "second trial" feature [75]. The *retry approach* cannot correct a permanent or persistent failure, but many studies have shown that many failures are of an intermittent nature. For example, a study revealed that 85% of the faults on relay computers were intermittent [65]. To be effective, the retry operation requires dynamic error detection (error detection within a very short time of its occurrence), and it also requires an undamaged copy of whatever information is necessary for the retry procedure. In the same spirit as the retry technique is the technique of *selective redundancy,* also called dynamic redundancy or spare-switching. As with the retry technique, selective redundancy requires good dynamic error detection and a valid copy of any necessary information so it can recover from the failure. Unlike the retry technique, the technique of selective redundancy can cope with a persistent failure. However, the application of selective redundancy requires knowledge of where the failure occurred so that the faulty unit can be switched out. Thus in selective redundancy, the basic approach is to supply redundant spare units tied to a common information and control bus, to switch out units in which a fault is located, and to switch in a good unit to take the place of the failed unit.

The application of *coding theory* to improve computer error control has been very successful. Codes are used not only for error detection, but also for error correction or fault masking. Codes have been most successfully applied to the transmission of information. Hsiao and Tou survey the use of error correcting codes in computers [76]. They cite impressive practical applications of these codes in main memory systems, magnetic tape units, disk file units, a photodigital storage unit, and a magnetic drum. They point out that codes are most useful when combined with other software and hardware redundancy techniques. Surveys of these redundancy techniques appear in the works of Short [77] and Avizienis [78].

The second problem related to internal checking is that of *fault diagnosis*. Chang *et al*. point out that fault masking does not work beyond the point where accumulated faults overwhelm the masking facility, and that in many applications the techniques of fault diagnosis plus repair is applicable [79]. In their book, an excellent presentation is made of automatic techniques to generate, select, and evaluate tests to diagnose digital systems. This subject is becoming increasingly crucial to computer system and logic designers.

Originally, when the replaceable unit was the vacuum tube or the basic electronic component, the primary aids of maintenance men were lists of diagnostic tests and fault signatures or dictionaries. Early approaches used a machine's instruction set to construct a diagnostic program. Diagnostic routines to locate faults predate electronic computers, since they were used on mechanical differential analyzers. In general, the engineers of early machines were satisfied if programs isolated the fault to the memory, an input–output unit, or the control or arithmetic unit [80].

Richards points out that for a diagnostic program to work, the computer had to be well enough "to get a program off the ground" [81]. The circuits that must be functioning to run a diagnostic program are called the *hard core*. Additional built-in checking circuits are also helpful (e.g., in the Whirlwind I, the trouble-location procedures centered on the built-in alarms). Eckert's experience with human faults and with diagnostic routines indicated that circuits used for fault-locating which were built right into the computer, were strongly recommended [64]. Today *diagnostic programming* or diagnostic microprogramming, in combination with hardware, has become more refined [82], as exemplified by the IBM System/360 Model 30 diagnostics which locate 90% of the gate failures [83]. As pointed out by Eldred [84], successful test routines depend on knowledge of the machine at the level of the components. This means that logic designers, or engineers familiar with the logic design of a machine, should write the diagnostic program or microprograms.

More recently, another approach called the *fault locating test* (FLT) has also been tried [85, 86]. Additional hardware is incorporated in the system to permit the application of a series of stimuli and to observe the corresponding responses. The FLTs are loaded into memory from an external medium. For each test, the data flow is initialized according to the stimulus pattern; a given number of machine cycles are run, and the result is compared with a known result. The primary sequence of tests is followed if no errors are found. If a primary test fails, and sufficient information is available to localize the fault, the result is displayed on the maintenance console. Otherwise further FLTs are applied in an attempt to improve the resolution.

Dent [87] points out there are two predominant levels of testing: *unit testing*, which checks individual units (such as an I/O unit, or even a printed circuit card) and *system testing*, which involves several units. Not only are there levels of testing to consider, but many environments are also involved: engineering, manufacturing, installation, and field maintenance [87]. Consequently, the manufacturing environment is assuming increased importance. Today, with the printed circuit card being the replaceable unit, acceptance tests for the card must be applied as it comes off the assembly line. As with simulation, automatic testing satisfies two purposes: it provides acceptance testing during manufacturing and assists maintenance of systems in the field. In the future, with larger scales of integration on semiconductor chips, manufacturing acceptance tests for these chips will become a much more difficult problem.

These considerations, addressed by Jones and Mays [88], show that the logic designer must now become concerned with the *testability* of his circuits [89, 90]. This point is also valid for the diagnosis problem and is considered by Chang *et al.* "To design a hardware system with no thought to diagnosability, and to then hand the frozen design to the fault diagnosis people, can only have one outcome. . . . Thus, there is real need for logic designers to become more familiar with diagnostic problems, and to work closely with the diagnosticians during the design of a system."†

Methods for analyzing circuits with faults have been developed; for example, Roth has devised the D algorithm [91], and Sellers *et al.* have defined the Boolean difference [70]. Langdon and Tang have used the Boolean difference to calculate the effectiveness of checking schemes on adder designs [92]. These techniques relate to the use of internal checking circuits, and indicate the strong relationship between internal checking and testing. Roth *et al.* describe an APL computer program called TEST-DETECT [93]. Bouricius *et al.* have used the interactive properties of this program in the design of logic circuits which are testable [94]. (A circuit is

† From H. Y. Chang, E. Manning, and G. Metze [79], "Fault Diagnosis of Digital Systems." © 1970, John Wiley & Sons, New York. Reprinted by permission of the publisher.

not testable if there exists some single gate failure for which there is no test to detect it, i.e., for which the circuit outputs behave normally; this may happen when the circuit has redundant gates.) The area of test generation is also of concern to logic design. The purpose of Seshu's "Sequential Analyser" program is to generate tests heuristically directly from a data file that contains the physical description of the computer's logic circuitry [49]. A test set is a set of tests that can detect all detectable single s-a-1 and s-a-0 faults.

A test set is always possible, in the "exhaustive" sense, but the problem is to achieve efficiently complete test sets that approach the minimum in size. The problem is tractable for combinational circuits, and the D algorithm [93] and Boolean difference [95] have been effectively employed for this purpose. A major problem exists in achieving reasonably sized test sets for circuits that contain flip-flops, i.e., sequential circuits. Approaches that treat the circuit as a sequential machine [96, 97] tend to produce too large a test set. An approach that holds promise has the logic designer utilizing techniques to enhance testability. Williams and Angell propose several schemes [98]. Roth notes the sequential system may utilize the D algorithm slightly modified if the logic designer uses a timing scheme he calls diagnosible design form [99]. The timing of the IBM S/360 Model 50 used this scheme, and Roth has determined that S/360 Models 40 and 195 also used this form. The algorithm for sequential circuits in diagnosible design form is called DALG5. In the future the logic designer will undoubtedly become more concerned with checking, testing, fault locating, and diagnosing. For this purpose, Chang *et al.* strongly recommend the strategy of using fault simulation during the detail design phase [79]. This strategy has been used with some success on the IBM System/370 Model 145 computer to test the effectiveness of diagnostic programs written in microcode. A discussion of simulation techniques related to fault detection appears in the book by Friedman and Menon [100, Chapter 5].

This section should end with a point that is sometimes overlooked. No matter how much redundancy is included in a computer, there is always a nonzero probability of an undetected machine error. It is not difficult or expensive to provide fair to good error coverage on single faults within the data flow, but protection against multiple faults becomes very expensive. In fact, the ability to detect many single errors in control logic, under the present state of the art, is very difficult, short of duplication and comparison. The designers of highly reliable computer systems for aerospace applications are well aware that the equipment put into a system to achieve the last few incremental improvements in reliability are very expensive.

9. Design Automation

The previous topics of design languages, simulation, and test generation pertain to the general area of design automation, i.e., the employment of data processing techniques to assist in the design of computers. The original job of the computer in design automation was in documentation, i.e., the keeping of wire lists and parts lists updated, the checking of fan-in and fan-out, and the drawing of block diagrams [101]. Currently, the computer may be used in many ways to assist the designer. Interactive graphics systems have been reported (e.g., Krosher and Sass [102]) for documentation and simulation. Systems also exist for the partitioning, component placement, and interconnection of the physical elements. A very good reference on the subject is a book edited by Breuer [103], in which Chapter 1 provides an introduction not only to design automation, but to the design process of a medium-to-large scale computer. Another general reference, with an excellent bibliography, is a survey paper by Breuer [104].

B. System Timing

1. The Machine Cycle and Micro-Operations

The material of this section is vital to the subject of logic design. The logic designer must be completely familiar with the digital machine's basic timing cycle or machine cycle and the relative placement of micro-operations within the cycle.

The heart of the digital computer is the machine cycle. Regarding machines with a central clock (the vast majority of present-day computers), the central clock generally provides a set of lines (typically from 4 to 12 lines). Each clock signal line carries its distinct wave form. These wave forms may be nonoverlapping such as the eight clock signals of the Whirlwind I, or they may overlap. Further, the clock signals may be thought of as pulses or as level signals, depending on the operation of the memory elements in the system. The duration of a machine cycle may be influenced by many factors. The worst-case delays encountered in the data flow for a micro-operation should not exceed the allotted time in the machine cycle. If the machine is controlled by a microprogram, the cycle time of the store where the microprogram resides may serve as a lower bound on the machine cycle duration. Many systems adjust the machine cycle, in some fashion, to the main memory cycle. In the Honeywell H-4200 Computer, for example, six machine cycles comprise one memory cycle.

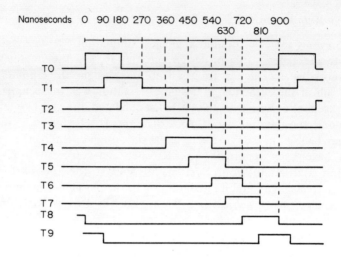

Fig. 3.2. IBM System/360 Model 25 overlapped timing signals.

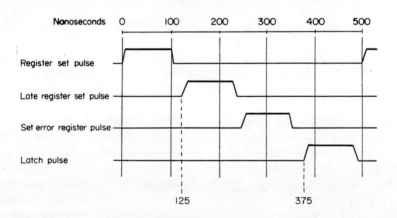

Fig. 3.3. IBM System/360 Model 50 nonoverlapped timing signals.

Examples of some machine cycle clock signals appear in Figs. 3.2 and 3.3. (For expository purposes, examples taken from actual computer designs are felt to be most useful here.) The adjacent overlapping signals of the System/360 Model 25 (Fig. 3.2) are used to achieve a more refined timing signal by gating two together in an AND gate. For example, signal $P1 = T0 \cdot T1$ provides a signal from 90-time to 180-time.

The four clock signals used in System/360 Model 50 (Fig. 3.3) are of interest because the system is basically two phase. During one phase, data generally flows from polarity hold flip-flops termed "latches" to polarity hold flip-flops called "registers," and during the other phase data passes from the "registers" through the arithmetic unit to the "latches."

The following appears in the book by Husson [105]. At 0-time to 100-time, under control of the Register Set Pulse, data from local store may be placed in a data flow register, as well as data from the adder output latches. Also at 0-time the new microinstruction appears from the read-only storage to control the machine cycle. Some of the microinstruction bits of the previous cycle need to be held over through 100-time because they determine the destination of data which is clocked into a register during Register Set Pulse (0–100). These bits are stored under control of the Late Register Set Pulse. The Set Error Register Pulse is used to sample some parity checks early enough in the cycle to stop the execution of the next microinstruction if an error is detected. The Latch Pulse is considered to be the second phase (where the Register Set Pulse is the first phase) and controls the transfer of the ALU (arithmetic and logical unit) result into the adder output latches. Also appearing at Latch Pulse time, if a memory Read Select was issued in a prior cycle, is information from the Storage Data Register. This is placed in the adder output latches for subsequent transfer during the next Register Set Pulse to one of the major data flow registers. Primary inputs to the system arrive at two times. Local Store data and control information are present at Register Set Pulse time, and data from main memory arrives at Latch Pulse time. System output for Local Store is from the registers and output for main memory is from the Adder Output Latches. The System/360 Model 50 operates with two clock phases as data is transferred from data flow registers to a "latch" at Latch Pulse time and then back to a data flow register at Register Set Pulse time. A simplified diagram of the operation is shown in Fig. 3.4.

Also of importance are the micro-operations that the data flow can perform. These are called "micro-orders" by the System/360 Model 50 machine designers. In simple parallel machines like the IBM 701, each instruction could consist of three to five machines cycles. For machines implementing more sophisticated architectures (involving effective address calculations, varied instruction and data formats, the use of both fixed point and floating point arithmetic, and the setting of status or condition codes), an instruction execution commonly comprises several machine cycles. For example, the average instruction execution time on the System/360 Model 30 is about 40 machine cycles. Thus in machine design, the execution of each instruction must be broken into a sequence of machine cycles, and each machine cycle must be broken into a sequence of micro-operations. In determining what happens in a particular machine cycle and scheduling the order of the cycles, the following points were made by Ware [106].

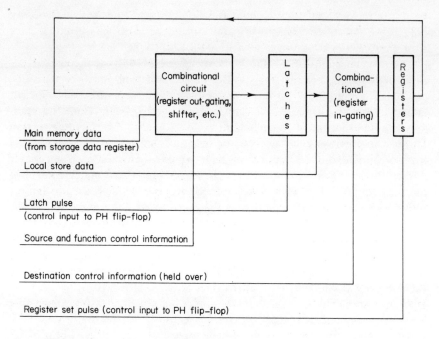

Fig. 3.4. Idealized model of IBM System/360 Model 50 data flow and timing.

(1) List each instruction and sequence of micro-operations that must occur.

(2) Construct a timing chart that schedules all micro-operations.

(3) Gather together micro-operations common to more than one instruction (for potential savings).

(4) Consider scheduling micro-operations in alternative or earlier times within the cycle.

(5) Reduce the cycle time if possible by doing some things concurrently.

(6) Juggle and rejuggle the timing charts to evolve a schedule of micro-operations for each instruction, thus compressing the time schedule to attain the fastest possible machine cycle.

As the development progresses, the period of the machine cycle may be more realistically measured because of more accurate estimates on worst-case times in delay chains. This might reschedule some micro-operations since the timing schedule must accommodate tolerances in the arrival time of signals.

The micro-operations are molded into a time frame. The worst-case delay chains do not always limit the machine cycle time. If the machine is microprogrammed, where one microinstruction controls one machine cycle, then the cycle time of the control memory that contains the microinstructions must be considered. The time to calculate the next microinstruction address may also limit machine cycle time; but perhaps of greater influence on the machine cycle is the main memory cycle time. In the IBM 1401, for example, both the machine cycle and main memory cycle were 11.5 microseconds. Typically a character that was read out of memory could be added to a character that had already been read out, and the result could be written back into memory. In the meantime, the address of the next character was routed to the memory address register.

Machine designers generally strive to "balance" the data flow cycle time and data paths widths with the timing of the control memory (if there is one), local store or scratch pad (if there is one), and main memory so that no one component is either overdesigned or is a bottleneck to internal performance. Thus many variables must be considered in selecting a machine cycle for a computer.

Once the timing charts are reconciled to a fixed, basic time interval and machine cycle, some reiteration or even rescheduling may be necessary. Implementation of the timing charts into logic is relatively straightforward. AND gates feeding OR gates are used as ingates which "funnel" data from many sources to a register or adder input; similarly, register or adder outputs may be placed on data buses for distribution.

To illustrate how micro-operations were juggled into place for the System/360 Model 25, the execution of a "Move/Arithemetic" type microinstruction is explained with the help of the timing chart of Fig. 3.2. At $T0$-time, the new microinstruction is placed in the control register and the microinstruction address is incremented. At $T1$-time, the local store is addressed by the bits in a particular field (A-field) of the microinstruction, and the byte is placed in the A-register. At $T3$-time, the local store is addressed by the bits of another field (B-field) of the microinstruction, and the byte is placed in the B-register. At $T5$-time, the next microinstruction address is placed in the address register and the Read Select signal is brought up. At $T8$-time, the one-byte arithmetic unit output is written into local store using the B-field address.

The methods of fixing the machine cycle described by Ware are usually not used in a serial machine design that uses serial-by-bit stores such as a delay line or drum for main memory. Shift registers, delay lines, and drums must be precisely clocked by bit-times, character (digit) times, and word times. In the case of drums, special timing tracks are used for character and word times. In these machines, the central data flow timing is entirely dependent on the timing of the memories.

For asynchronous control, instructions are nevertheless executed by a sequence of micro-operations. As in clocked systems, the asynchronous micro-operations are listed and grouped together to minimize equipment. The micro-operations report the end of their activity by a completion signal. The time scale is more pliable than in systems with a basic timing cycle. Micro-operations can be inserted, deleted, or modified in a sequence of micro-operations without causing much disruption.

In present practice, the period of the machine cycle is also the cycle time of the data flow. For example, in one machine cycle the System/360 Model 50 can gate the contents of two registers through the adder, shift the result, and place it back into one of the registers. In some clocked systems it is possible not to have a fixed period; i.e., under certain circumstances a "long" or "short" machine cycle may be forced. The RCA Spectra 70 Model 45 has a basic cycle of 480 nanoseconds but for two special types of microinstructions, the cycle time becomes 720 nanoseconds so that two adder cycles may be accommodated [105]. In systems that use job completion signaling, the duration of a data flow cycle becomes hazy; however, this cycle still exists since machine designers tend to structure the data flow to do a basic or typical sequence of micro-operations.

Ware mentions the possibility of a mixed system, where one part might be synchronized by a clock and another part might use job completion signals. Instead of interpreting an "event" to be a fundamental micro-operation, it might be interpreted to be a collection of micro-operations or a lengthy sequence which loops. Ware [106] feels the job completion signal philosophy might be the appropriate way to design a "supercontrol" unit which coordinates entire machines and devices.

2. Clocking Configurations

Chu defines *clocking configuration* as the means by which information is transferred from one set of flip-flops to another in a clocked system and feels the proper selection is very important, involving consideration of the circuit switching speeds, signal line lengths, and cost [1]. He presents examples of four such configurations. The general model is shown in Fig. 3.5,

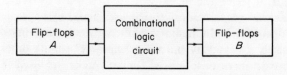

Fig. 3.5. Clocking configuration.

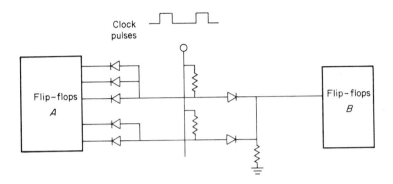

Fig. 3.6. A clocking and powering configuration.

where information is transferred from the flip-flops A to flip-flops B. In this first example of a clocking configuration, a clock pulse at flip-flops A causes a pulse to be generated and sent through the "combinational circuit" to the inputs of flip-flops B. In the second example, similar to the Whirlwind I configuration, the flip-flops provide a level output; a clock pulse is applied to the input of the "combinational circuit" and combined with the level signals through AND gates to provide a pulse into flip-flops B. The third scheme (Fig. 3.6) shows clocking and power combined into one function [107].

In the fourth arrangement, flip-flops A provide level signals which are combined in the combinational logic circuit to provide a level conditioning signal into flip-flops B. This level signal is clocked into the flip-flop, as in the diode gate system of the IBM 702 and IBM 705 computers.

3. The Earle Classifications

In 1961, Earle [108] observed three levels of digital systems design:

(1) the *combinational logic circuit* level (AND, OR, NOT, NOR, etc.),
(2) the *sequential circuit* level, and
(3) the *sequential system* level.

At the combinational logic level, the circuits may be *pulse* circuits or *level* circuits. Earle subdivides pulse circuits into (a) dc coupled or (b) ac coupled (see Fig. 3.7), whereas all level circuits are dc coupled. Systems need not use pulses or levels exclusively.

At the sequential circuit level, Earle describes synchronous and asynchronous operation. In synchronous operation the clock pulses provide the timing; synchronous operation may be of two types: pulse or level. In

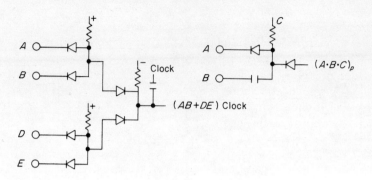

Fig. 3.7. Pulse combinational circuits.

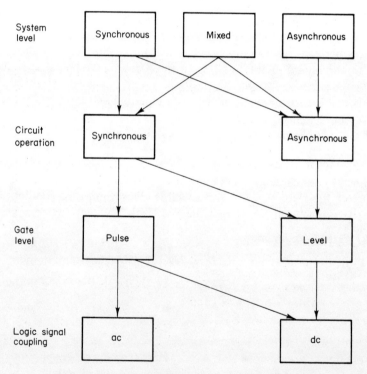

Fig. 3.8. The logic and timing classifications of Earle [108].

the case of synchronous level operation, Earle observes that the timed relationship is between input control signals. In synchronous circuits this often results in multiphase clock signals; overlapping, nonoverlapping, and sometimes with different pulse widths [108].

In describing asynchronous sequential circuit operation, Earle states the fundamental mode assumption, i.e., allowing the circuit to become stable before changing its inputs, but also states the next operation is initiated as a function of the previous one.

Sequential systems are too complex to be treated as a single sequential circuit for two reasons: (1) the large number of variables involved and (2) the large number of design alternatives. The system is broken into smaller interconnected units by synchronous or asynchronous means, or by a mixture. Earle points out that synchronous circuits can use timing signals to coordinate or "uncouple" these units, the alternative is to generate job invitation and job completion control signals to provide the proper sequencing [108]. In an example of asynchronous system operation, Earle uses three values encoded with two signal lines, the double-rail technique of Sims and Gray [109], to form three values: 0, 1, or N (nothing). Earle feels the most common system is the mixed synchronous–asynchronous type, where the memory and data flow are synchronous, and input/output equipment are interconnected to the system by means of job initiation and job completion signaling. Figure 3.8 shows how Earle relates the system, circuit, and gate design levels.

4. A Classification of Logic and Timing Configurations

Chu [1] has studied clocking configurations and Earle has studied logic and timing schemes [108]. Chapter 1 described some actual logic and timing schemes, and Chapter 2 attempted to classify and model the many kinds of circuits and timing schemes encountered in digital systems. This section presents a more encompassing definition of a *logic and timing configuration*: it is defined as the means by which the (1) sequence of input states, (2) the memory elements, and (3) the system timing scheme are interrelated to implement the specifications for a functional unit or system of functional units within a digital system. In the past, the terms asynchronous, synchronous, fundamental mode, pulse mode, clocked input, level input and level output have been intended to describe various logic and timing schemes.

The terms *asynchronous* and *synchronous* are ambiguous because no single term is adequate to describe a logic and timing configuration. It is not useful to attempt to classify all schemes as belonging to one of these two classes. Earle has approached the classification problem by dividing a system into levels and providing classifications for each level. The author has refined Earle's general approach and has divided the system aspects into three categories. These categories are described in the following three subsections.

a. The Input Sequence

There are two basic ways to view the input sequence to a sequential circuit. The essential characteristic that differentiates them is whether or not "like successive inputs" are permitted, i.e., whether input state x_i is permitted to follow the same input state x_i. (Recall that in fundamental mode circuits, once a stable state is achieved, only an input state change can cause another internal state change; hence, an input state does not follow itself in the input sequence.) For like successive inputs, there must exist a null (spacer) input state, or some clock (timing) signal, or a redundant input signal encoding, to distinguish between successive occurrences of the same input state. Therefore, it is useful to view schemes where like successive inputs are permitted as possessing a "spacer" input state, and these schemes are said to operate in *pulse-input* mode. A sequential machine described by a Mealy or Moore flow table operates in pulse-input mode. Alternatively, schemes where each input signal change signifies a new input state may be described by a Huffman flow table and are said to operate in *level-input* mode. The Mealy and Moore flow tables may be converted to a Huffman flow table by making the mechanism of the "spacer" input explicit; this permits like successive inputs. Thus, the Mealy and Moore descriptions can be viewed as being a level of abstraction above the Huffman flow table because of the additional simplifying assumptions.

One method of treating inputs to a digital system is to combine the pulse-input and level-input mode. Here the signals are all level inputs, including a plurality of signals coming from a clock. Some memory elements of the system may change state on the rise of a clock signal, while others may change on the fall. In this sense the system recognizes level inputs; however, at the machine cycle level, inputs other than the internal clock are presented only once per machine cycle. If the system is observed at the machine cycle level, then like successive external inputs are permitted, and with these inputs the system is usefully viewed as operating on a pulse-input basis. With this example the comment that pulse-mode is a level of abstraction above level-input mode should be more meaningful.

b. Binary Memory Elements

The technology of the memory element and its mode of operation determines to a large extent the logic and timing configuration used in a computer system. (For example, the SEAC mode of operation revolved around the dynamic flip-flop.) A binary memory element is a single output sequential circuit that can store no more than one bit of information; i.e., the flow table description of the circuit has no more than two stable states for any input state. Many binary memory elements have a second output line which is the complement of the "true" output.

Now an attempt will be made to identify some basic types of binary memory elements. This classification is not claimed to be all encompassing, but it does cover all binary memory elements encountered in this work. The *nonlogic clocked* memory elements use a special nonlogic signal applied directly to the memory element for their operation. This clocking signal is never combined with the logic signals in the system. Examples of these elements are the pulse power signal of four-phase field-effect transistor (FET) logic, the phased pump supply of the phase-locked oscillator, the "sync" and "clamp" signals of the Havens delay unit, and the sine wave of the SEAC dynamic flip-flop. This class of memory element motivated the synchronous classification of sequential circuits. A system composed of these memory elements changes state in synchronism with the special nonlogic signal. We note here that binary counters of the ripple-carry type cannot be built from this kind of memory element.

Pulse-sensitive memory elements require the application of a controlled pulse to the memory element, but this pulse can also be combined logically with other logic signals in the system. This type of memory element was used in the ENIAC and Whirlwind I. With a pulse reshaping circuit like the gated pulse amplifier, this memory element can be used to build a ripple-carry binary counter. Both this memory element and the nonlogic clocked memory element have the property observed by Phister and Caldwell, i.e., making one type of memory element behave like another by the addition of suitable combinational circuits. A shift register can also be implemented with these memory elements, using one element per bit.

The *edge-sensitive* memory element changes state due to a change in the logic signal level at an input. The change in level to which this memory element responds is either a rising edge (0-to-1) or falling edge (1-to-0), but not both. The element provides a level output and is sensitive to rise or fall times but not to a pulse width. Edge-sensitive memory elements in the past have used a resistor–diode–capacitor gate to convert a change in levels to a triggering pulse. In Fig. 1.21 an important class of edge-sensitive memory elements is shown which does not use ac coupling and therefore is easily implemented in integrated circuits. In defining this class, the class of flip-flops used in the IAS computer will be excluded.

It is difficult to define precisely an edge-sensitive binary memory element; nevertheless, the author feels the following definition is useful. An edge-sensitive flip-flop is a binary memory element that does not have a special nonlogic input, has an essential hazard in its Huffman flow table description, and has no maximum pulse-width constraint on any input signal. Also note that all edge-sensitive memory elements that have been previously discussed can, by the addition of a combinational circuit at its inputs, behave like a toggle, i.e., perform the single-stage binary counter function.

Smith and Roth, who studied edge-sensitive flip-flops [110], defined two classes of flip-flop inputs: the level inputs and edge inputs. The flip-flop can change output state only on one of the transitions (rising or falling) of an edge input. They note that "hidden" states exist in these devices; i.e., the next output cannot always be determined from knowledge of the present input state and output state alone. They illustrate several kinds of edge-sensitive flip-flops; their definition of the unclocked RS flip-flop that has no hidden states is the only definition that does not conform to ours. (We consider this latter type of RS flip-flop to be "level-sensitive," as opposed to edge-sensitive.)

It is possible, with edge-sensitive toggle flip-flops, to implement the binary ripple-carry counter. It is generally not possible, however, by the addition of combinational circuits, to make one edge-sensitive element look like any other in its class. For example, a single-input edge-sensitive toggle cannot be made to appear like an edge-sensitive (two-input) JK flip-flop even though by tying the J and K inputs together the JK behaves like a toggle. The JK flip-flop cannot be made to appear like the very general and more powerful inhibited-toggle flip-flop defined by Smith and Roth [110]. As pointed out by McCluskey, edge-sensitive flip-flops can serve as replacements for pulse-sensitive flip-flops. This is the way these memory elements were applied in the IBM 702 and IBM 705 computers. However, the edge-sensitive flip-flop is more powerful and can be used in many other ways, particularly in circuits using mainly level logic signals. The application of a single-input edge-sensitive toggle flip-flop as an element of a one flip-flop per stage shift register depends on the memory element delay versus the delay of a two-level AND–OR combinational circuit.

The *level-sensitive* or gate-type memory element is basically a binary memory element using level logic signal inputs whose behavioral description does not have an essential hazard. These elements can generally be described by a Huffman flow table with two internal states. The IBM 650 latch and the cross-coupled NOR or NAND flip-flops fall into this category. Obviously by the addition of suitable combinational logic, one of these memory elements can be made to look like another in the class; however, stray delay considerations will change. A binary ripple-carry counter cannot be built using one of these flip-flops per stage, nor can a shift register be designed using only a single memory element per bit with this class of memory element. This is because the Huffman flow table description of a shift register stage or a binary counter unit has four internal states and not two. Pulse-sensitive or edge-sensitive memory elements can realize the counter or shifter functions on a "one-memory-element-per-bit" basis because of the existence of the "hidden" internal states. Level-sensitive memory elements were used in the IAS computer; this effort resulted in the "double rank" concept of Bigelow, where counters and shifters were implemented with two level-sensitive memory elements per bit.

In his book, Maley [111] constructs many memory elements from combinational gates. Some of the elements have the edge-sensitive property and in order to be "reliable" in operation (to operate without a hazard) the gate delays must exceed the line delays. Except for the set-dominant SR flip-flop, the level-sensitive flip-flops have only two internal states, i.e., they only have one feedback loop.

The *delay element* is not a bistable binary memory element by itself, but can be combined with combinational decision elements to form a nonlogic pulsed element (e.g., the SEAC dynamic flip-flop or Havens delay unit). In present practice, the delay element is rarely found in feedback loops of level logic sequential circuits; this is contrary to what is found in the theoretical literature. The delay element may be viewed as an element with three internal states: stable in the 0-state, stable in the 1-state, and unstable in a transient state. The Huffman flow table for the element is shown in Fig. 3.9. (Note that in the table entry, the next-state and the output state are separated by a comma.) The length of time the element spends in state 2, the transient state, is the value of the delay. In practice, delay elements are used in clock circuits to derive phased clock pulses from a single clock pulse source; examples also include use as "time-outs" for various opera-

	Input	
State	0	1
0	0, 0	2, 0
1	2, 1	1, 1
2	0, 1	1, 0

Fig. 3.9. Flow table of delay element.

TABLE 3.2.   Logic and Timing Configurations

---

(1) Input sequence
  (a) Pulse-input
  (b) Level-input

(2) Binary memory elements
  (a) Nonlogic clocked
  (b) Pulse-sensitive
  (c) Edge-sensitive
  (d) Level-sensitive
  (e) Delay element

(3) System timing
  (a) Invitation and job completion signalling
  (b) Central clock
  (c) Mixed

---

tions, and use in control logic for electromechanical devices to provide proper width driver signals. Delay elements in the past have been used in accumulators (see Chu [1]) and between stages of a shift register constructed from level-sensitive flip-flops.

Signals are often brought into a digital system from mechanical contacts. The contacts may "bounce," i.e., the signal may experience a period of fluctuation between the 1-state and the 0-state, instead of opening or closing smoothly. In cases where a normally open and normally closed contact are both provided, the contact bounce problem is easily solved (see e.g., Maley [111]). However, with only a single contact, the signal must be brought into the system by a circuit that uses a delay element whose value exceeds the bounce time. Delay elements can be used with combinational gates to build a single-shot multivibrator circuit. The single-shot or one-shot circuit will provide an output pulse of a given width upon the rise (or fall, depending on the design) of its input.

c. System Timing

Earle has shown that there are two basic kinds of system timing methods: the use of clocking signals and the use of invitation and job completion signals. A third approach is to mix these two methods. Earle points out that clocking signals uncouple sequential circuits from each other. Certain memory elements change state only at a given clock signal; other sets of memory elements change at other clock signals. At the system (global) level (not the sequential circuit level), the fundamental mode notion, i.e., the notion that inputs should not be changed while the circuit is not internally stable, is violated many times in practice. For example, in the System/360 Model 50, inputs to the combinational circuit that feed the registers may be changing while the latches are changing state (see Fig. 3.4).

The various types of memory elements, inputs, and system timings, are shown in Table 3.2. These types can be combined in many ways. Generally, systems with the nonlogic clocked memory elements operate in the clocked system mode. The use of a clock signal often implies the pulse-input mode for the input sequence; however, the overall system timing can be controlled by job completion signaling as in the NAREC computer. Further, the inputs other than the nonlogic clock signal could operate in the level-input mode. Thus, four-phase MOS FET technology can be used to implement the control of a building's elevator system, where many of the primary inputs, people pushing buttons, are not clocked.

The use of a particular kind of memory element in a system does not preclude the use of others. Delay, edge-sensitive, and level-sensitive memory elements are commonly used in the same digial system. In the first two chapters of this review, a large variety of schemes, circuit technology, and models have been encountered. Therefore, the existence of a large variety of logic and timing configurations should not be viewed with surprise. The logic designer, however, sometimes does not have a choice in the technology he is to use in implementing a system; consequently, logic designers are interested in determining what can be done with a given set of building blocks. This is the subject of the next section.

5. Systems of Circuit Logic

Braun defines a *system of circuit logic* as a compatible set of components that may realize any sequential circuit in a computer [112]. Gray addressed the problem of determining, in a systematic manner, whether a proposed set of switching and storage circuits was a system of circuit logic; the answer he found was that we have a creative art which at that time was not reduced to a science [113]. Gray then provided a review and classification of prior art. Braun also discussed some of the more outstanding systems of circuit logic. In this section, we address the adequacy of certain sets of building blocks.

First one must have the ability to construct combinational circuits; i.e., there must be combinational or decision elements. At least one element type must have a fan-out greater than one. If memory elements are to be constructed from these combinational circuits, then signal amplification is needed because the feedback loops must contain greater than unity gain. (For example, one cannot construct a level-sensitive SR flip-flop from diode AND and OR gates because the feedback loop would contain less than unity gain.)

In some cases the memory elements provide both signal amplification and complementation. A combinational circuit can be synthesized with only AND and OR gates, provided both polarities of the inputs are provided. If the memory elements provide both true and complement outputs with adequate power, then diode AND and OR gates are sufficient for the combinational aspects of synthesis, provided all primary inputs have complements.

The sequential aspects of synthesis do not always revolve around the hazardfree design of Huffman flow tables. One can, for example, build a computer from elements that are not sufficient to realize any arbitrary Huffman flow table, provided multiple phase clock signals are available. In fact, a very common and simple combination sufficient to construct the logic of a computer is the use of a multiphase clock source, combinational circuit elements, and level-sensitive flip-flops constructed from these gates. Thus, all computer logic can be performed with a two-phase clock and transistor NOR elements. Recall that the System/360 Model 50 data flow is organized on this principle. Memory elements changed by one phase of the clock signal should not feed memory elements timed by the same phase, and the time between clock signals should be sufficient to perform the required amount of combinational logic. Primary inputs to the system should be timed so they are stable inputs during the desired clock signal.

A single clock pulse may be fed through delay elements to provide a multiphased clock. Alternatively, the clock may be used as the input to a ring counter or Gray-coded counter to provide a source of clock signals. In the latter case, the counter function possesses an essential hazard; consequently, some means, perhaps even constraints on stray delays, must exist to avoid this hazard. In general, the circuit that provides the multiphased timing signals must be designed according to classic synthesis procedures.

When the clock is single-phased, then all memory elements probably change at the same time or within a short period following the changing clock signal. Some means must exist within the circuit to avoid hazards. If the memory elements are of the nonlogic clocked, pulse-sensitive, or edge-sensitive kind, then the response time of the memory elements, possibly in combination with the pulse width, provide protection against hazards.

In a single-phase clock system with level-sensitive memory elements, care must be taken to avoid races and steady-state hazards. Depending on the delay assumptions, it may be necessary to use delay elements. In practice, however, once a requirement to use delay elements in a single-phase system develops, more often a single delay is used to achieve a second clock or timing signal in certain areas. Note that this differs from the theoretical methods of using many delays in memory element feedback loops.

When the system is unclocked, then some kind of completion signal must be provided to indicate the circuit is ready for another input. If the circuit is known always to respond faster than its inputs change, then an explicit job completion signal is not needed. In unclocked level-input systems where a completion signal is not required, the Huffman flow table synthesis procedures apply (in this application particular attention should be given to races and hazards). When the memory elements are the level-sensitive type, then depending on the delay assumptions, delay elements may be needed. If the circuit inputs are pulses that drive pulse-sensitive or edge-sensitive memory elements, and a gated pulse amplifier element is available, the procedures (see Chapter 2) described by Caldwell apply. Level-input mode, unclocked circuits using edge-sensitive flip-flops for memory elements have hardly been investigated, but the realization procedures appear to be comparable to those for the class of level-input unclocked circuits using level-sensitive memory elements.

For schemes where the unclocked level-input mode is combined with job completion signaling, the work described in Chapter 2 by Muller and others involved in the Illiac II applies. They have shown that combinational gates and level-sensitive flip-flops constructed from them are adequate building blocks, provided stray line delays do not exceed stray gate delays. In certain areas, such as fan-out trees, an additional assumption was required: the ratio of best-case to worst-case gate delay did not exceed about eight.

Up to this point, the logic discussed has been the internal logic of a computer. However, digital systems must interface with the outside. To do this, a class of circuits called "special" circuits (as opposed to "logic" circuits) are required. This class of circuits include indicator drivers, line drivers, voltage converting circuits, oscillators, single-shots, delay lines, Schmitt triggers, and sense amplifiers; however, the need for these circuits varies with the application. Delay elements play an important role in interface logic. Pulse widths of specific durations are often required, for example, to drive electromechanical equipment and to provide precisely controlled timing within a read–write memory cycle. Many applications require the interfacing of a current circuit technology with an older technology. This is accomplished through "mixer" circuits, which convert logic levels and impedances of one technology to another.

The question of the adequacy of a "system of circuit logic" may depend partly on the timing scheme and partly on delay assumptions. The author knows of no references where this problem is studied in depth. In his superb text, which covers many practical points,† Peatman [114] studies

---

† This text is highly recommended for its "real-world" flavor.

TABLE 3.3.   Systems of Circuit Logic

---

(1) Combinational elements (with amplification somewhere)
    (a) AND, OR, NOT
    (b) NOR
    (c) NAND
    (d) AND, OR, double-rail logic

(2) Sequential circuits
    (a) Combinational elements and multiphased clock (clocked funda-
         mental mode)
    (b) Single-phased clock and edge- or pulse-sensitive memory elements
    (c) Multiphased clock and mixed edge-sensitive and level-sensitive
         memory elements
    (d) Single-phased clock, delay elements, and combinational elements
    (e) Combinational elements, some delay constraints, job completion
         signalling

---

several clocking schemes, primarily in the context of edge-sensitive memory elements. Some schemes are summarized in Table 3.3.

C. A Summary of Current Design Practice

In general terms, logic design practice has not changed greatly since the first generation; the good design techniques of today were valid in the first generation. The "divide and conquer" approach is used where the machine is divided into functional units and functional units are further subdivided. For computer systems, the data flow, or structural component, is important; it consists of the central registers, arithmetic unit, and data paths that interconnect them. The main memory also interfaces with the data flow, as may input–output busses. The data flow is caused to behave properly during the symbolic design phase by means of organizing and sequencing micro-operations. This may be done by a microprogram in control memory or by "hard-wired" logic. The sequencing of the micro-operations is an integral part of the system timing. The basic cycle of a clocked data flow is generally called the machine cycle. The timing of the machine sometimes depends on the memory element used for the registers. The use of polarity-hold flip-flops requires a multiphased clock and that all data "loops" have at least two flip flops. On the other hand, the use of edge-sensitive flip-flops permits "data loops" of only one flip-flop. (This may be the case for an adder carry flip-flop.) The three key aspects that must be fairly well resolved before entering the detailed design phase are (1) the data flow, (2) the micro-operations (and their sequencing), and (3) the timing (machine cycle or logic and timing configuration). These three areas are interrelated and some iterations may take place. In the detailed design phase, the machine logic is designed down to the basic gate and flip-flop level. The gates must be packaged, i.e., assigned to modules and printed circuit card locations and interconnected. Subsidiary activities include simulation, checking against packaging and wiring rules, and the generation of tests and diagnostics.

References

1. Y. Chu, "Digital Computer Design Fundamentals." McGraw-Hill, New York, 1962.
2. H. Hellerman, "Digital Computer System Principles." McGraw-Hill, New York, 1967 (2nd ed., 1973).
3. V. L. Hesse, The advantages of logical equation techniques in designing digital computers. *Proc. AFIPS, Western Joint Comput. Conf., Los Angeles, California, May 6-8, 1958*, **13**, pp. 186–188.
4. D. L. Moon, Digital machine design and analysis. *Comput. Design* **9** (7), 59–65 (1970).
5. G. M. Amdahl, Logical design method. *Proc. AFIPS, Western Joint Comput. Conf., Los Angeles, California, May 6-8, 1958*, **13**, p. 176.
6. L. S. Bensky, Block diagrams in logic design. *Proc. AFIPS, Western Joint Comput. Conf., Los Angeles, California, May 6-8, 1958*, **13**, pp. 177–178.
7. R. K. Richards, Logical design methods. *Proc. AFIPS, Western Joint Comput. Conf., Los Angeles, California, May 6-8, 1958*, **13**, pp. 179–181.
8. H. L. Engel, Machine language in digital computer design. *Proc. AFIPS, Western Joint Comput. Conf., Los Angeles, California, May 6-8, 1958*, **13**, pp. 182–186.
9. F. B. Cole and S. E. Zimmerman, Self-repair techniques investigation. *Clearinghouse Rep. AD-657-247*. NTIS, Springfield, Virginia 22151, 1967.
10. S. P. Frankel, The logical design of a simple general purpose computer. *IRE Trans. Electron. Comput.* **EC-6**, 5–14 (1957).
11. G. P. Dinneen, I. L. Lebow, and I. S. Reed, The logical design of CG24. *Proc. AFIPS Eastern Joint Comput. Conf., Philadelphia, Pennsylvania, December 1958*, **14**, pp. 91–94.
12. E. Glaser, Cascaded variable cycle control as applied to the 220 computer. *Proc. AFIPS, Western Joint Comput. Conf., Los Angeles, California, May 6-8, 1958*, **13**, pp. 63–65.
13. J. Hudson, W. Edwards, and D. E. Eckdahl, The flow diagram approach to computer logical design using the NCR 304 as an illustration. *Proc. AFIPS, Western Joint Comput. Conf., Los Angeles, California, May 6-8, 1958*, **13**, pp. 59–62.
14. M. V. Wilkes, Microprogramming. *Proc. AFIPS Eastern Joint Comput. Conf., Philadelphia, Pennsylvania, December 1958*, **14**, pp. 18–20.
15. M. V. Wilkes, The growth of interest in microprogramming. *Comput. Surveys* **1**, 139–145 (1969).
16. J. J. Eachus, Logical organization of the Honeywell H-290. *Trans. Amer. Inst. Elec. Eng. Part I* **79**, 715–719 (1961).
17. T. C. Bartee, I. L. Lebow, and I. S. Reed, "Theory and Design of Digital Machines." McGraw-Hill, New York, 1962.
18. G. C. Vandling and D. E. Waldecker, The microprogram control technique for digital logic design. *Comput. Design* **8** (8), 44–51 (1969).

19. R. F. Rosin, Contemporary concepts of microprogramming and emulation. *Comput. Surveys* **1**, 197–212 (1969).
20. Flow charting techniques. IBM Data Process. Techn. Doc., Form No. GC20-8152. IBM, 1971. (Available from IBM Branch Offices.)
21. H. H. Goldstine and J. von Neumann, "Planning and Coding Problems for an Electronic Computing Instrument," Vols. I, II, III. Van Nostrand-Reinhold, Princeton, New Jersey, 1947 and 1948.
22. R. E. Swartwout, One method of designing speed-independent logic for a control. *Proc. Annu. Symp. Switching Circuit Theory and Logical Design, 2nd, Detroit, Michigan, October 1961*, AIEE Publ. **S-134**, pp. 94–105.
23. R. E. Swartwout, New techniques for designing speed independent control logic. *Proc. Annu. Symp. Switching Circuit Theory and Logical Design, 5th, Princeton, New Jersey, October 1964*, IEEE Publ. **S-164**, pp. 12–29.
24. D. B. Gillies, A flow chart notation for the description of a speed-independent control. *Proc. Annu. Symp. Switching Circuit Theory and Logical Design, 2nd, Detroit, Michigan, October 1961*, AIEE Publ. **S-134**, pp. 105–110.
25. R. E. Miller, "Switching Theory," Vol. 2. Wiley, New York, 1966.
26. S. Gorn, P. Z. Ingerman, and J. B. Crozier, On the construction of micro-flowcharts. *Comm. ACM* **2**, 27–31 (1960).
27. D. H. Rutherford, A systematic design technique for digital systems. IBM Rep. TR 01.01.001.632. IBM, Endicott, New York, February 20, 1962.
28. A. MacKinnon, Flow chart methods of logic design. *Comput. Design* **7** (2), 72–75 (1968).
29. Y. Chu, "Introduction to Computer Organization." Prentice-Hall, Englewood Cliffs, New Jersey, 1970.
30. H. R. Hartson, Digital control simulation system. *Proc. Annu. Design Automation Workshop, 6th, Miami Beach, Florida, June 1969*, pp. 113–128. ACM, New York, 1969.
31. D. F. Gorman and J. P. Anderson, A logic design translator. *Proc. AFIPS Fall Joint Comput. Conf., Philadelphia, Pennsylvania, 1962*, **22**, pp. 251–261.
32. R. M. Proctor, A logic design translator experiment demonstrating relationships of language to systems and logic design. *IEEE Trans. Comput.*, **EC-13**, 422–430 (1964).
33. D. F. Gorman, System level design automation. *Annu. IEEE Comput. Conf., 1st, Chicago, Illinois, September 1967*, Digest, IEEE Publ. **16 C51**, pp. 131–134.
34. K. E. Iverson, "A Programming Language." Wiley, New York, 1962.
35. K. E. Iverson, A programming language. *Proc. AFIPS, Spring Joint Comput. Conf., San Francisco, California, 1962*, **21**, pp. 345–351.
36. A. D. Falkoff, K. E. Iverson, and E. H. Sussenguth, Formal description of system/360. *IBM Syst. J.* **3**, 198–262 (1964).
37. C. G. Bell and A. Newell, The PMS and ISP descriptive systems for computer structures. *Proc. AFIPS Spring Joint Comput. Conf., 1970*, **36**, pp. 351–374. AFIPS Press, Montvale, New Jersey, 1970.
38. T. D. Friedman and S. C. Yang, Methods used in an automatic logic design generator (ALERT). *IEEE Trans. Comput.* **C-18**, 593–614 (1969).
39. Y. Chu, An ALGOL-like computer design language. *Comm. ACM* **8**, 607–615 (1965).
40. B. D. McCurdy and Y. Chu, Boolean translation of a macro logic design. *Annu. IEEE Comput. Conf., 1st, September 1967*, Digest, IEEE Publ. **16 C51**, pp.124–127.
41. H. Schorr, Computer-aided digital system design and analysis using a register transfer language. *IEEE Trans. Comput.* **EC-13**, 730–737 (1964).
42. H. Schlaeppi, A formal language for describing machine logic, timing and sequencing (LOTIS). *IEEE Trans. Comput.* **EC-13**, 439–448 (1964).

43. G. Metze and S. Seshu, A proposal for a computer compiler. *Proc. Spring Joint Comput. Conf., 1966,* **29,** 253–263. Spartan, Washington, D.C., 1966.
44. J. R. Duley and D. L. Dietmeyer, A digital system design language (DDL). *IEEE Trans. Comput.* **C-17,** 850–860 (1968).
45. J. R. Duley and D. L. Dietmeyer, Translation of a DDL digital system specification to Boolean equations, *IEEE Trans. Comput.* **C-18,** 305–313 (1969).
46. M. A. Breuer, General survey of design automation of digital computers. *Proc. IEEE* **54,** 1708–1721 (1966).
47. A. R. McKay, Comment on 'computer-aided design: Simulation of digital design logic.' *IEEE Trans. Comput.* **C-18,** 362 (1969).
48. D. W. Lake, Logic simulation in digital systems. *Comput. Design* **9** (8), 77–83 (1970).
49. S. Seshu and D. Freeman, The diagnosis of asynchronous sequential switching systems. *IRE Trans. Comput.* **EC-11,** 459–465 (1962).
50. M. A. Breuer, Techniques for the simulation of computer logic. *Comm. ACM* **7,** 443–446 (1964).
51. P. W. Case, H. H. Graff, L. E. Griffith, A. R. LeClerq, W. B. Murley, and T. M. Spence, Solid logic design automation for IBM System/360. *IBM J. Res. Develop.* **8,** 127–140 (1964).
52. E. G. Ulrich, Time-sequenced logical simulation based on circuit delay and selective tracing of active network paths. *Proc. ACM Nat. Conf., Cleveland, Ohio, 1965,* pp. 437–447.
53. E. G. Ulrich, Exclusive simulation of activity in digital networks. *Comm. ACM* **12,** 102–110 (1969).
54. Y. T. Yen, A mathematical model characterizing four-phase MOS circuits for logic simulation. *IEEE Trans. Comput.* **C-17,** 822–826 (1968).
55. L. Shalla, Automatic analysis of electronic digital circuits using list processing. *Comm. ACM* **9,** 372–380 (1966).
56. E. B. Eichelberger, Hazards detection in combinational and sequential switching circuits. *IBM J. Res. Develop.* **9,** 90–99 (1965).
57. J. S. Jephson, R. P. McQuarrie, and R. E. Vogelsberg, A three-value computer design verification system. *IBM Syst. J.* **8,** 178–188 (1969).
58. G. G. Langdon, Jr., Analysis of asynchronous circuits under different delay assumptions. *IEEE Trans. Comput.* **C-17,** 1131–1143 (1968).
59. S. H. Unger, Hazards and delays in asynchronous sequential switching circuits. *IRE Trans. Circuit Theory* **CT-6,** 12–25 (1959).
60. L. H. Tung, A unit delay logic timing simulator. IBM Tech. Rep. TD 01.509. IBM, Endicott, New York, October 30, 1969.
61. D. L. Smith, Models and data structures for digital logic simulation. MSEE Thesis, MIT, Cambridge, Massachusetts, June 1966. (Available from NTIS, Springfield, Virginia 22151 under accession number AD637192.)
62. E. G. Manning and H. Y. Chang, A comparison of fault simulation methods for digital systems. *Annu. IEEE Comput. Conf., 1st, Chicago, Illinois, September 1967,* Digest, IEEE Publ. **16 C51,** pp. 10–13.
63. E. G. Manning and H. Y. Chang, Functional techniques for efficient digital simulation. *IEEE Int. Conv. Digest, New York, 1968* p. 194.
64. J. P. Eckert, Jr., Checking circuits and diagnostic routines. *IRE Nat. Conv. Rec.* **1,** P. 7, 62–65 (1953).
65. Eng. Res. Assoc., "High-Speed Computing Devices." McGraw-Hill, New York, 1950.
66. J. W. Mauchly, The advantages of built-in checking, *Proc. AFIPS Eastern Joint Comput. Conf., Washington, D.C., 1953,* **4,** pp. 99–101.

67. J. P. Eckert, Jr., J. R. Weiner, H. F. Welsh, and H. F. Mitchell, The UNIVAC system. *Rev. Electron. Digital Comput. Joint AIEE-IRE Comput. Conf., December 1951,* AIEE Special Publ. S-44, pp. 6–16.

68. W. Buchholz, The system design of the IBM Type 701 computer. *Proc. IRE* **41,** 1262–1275 (1953).

69. D. E. Waldecker and R. Schoenfeld, IBM Fed. Syst. Div., private communication, 1970.

70. F. F. Sellers, Jr., M. Y. Hsiao, and L. W. Bearnson, "Error Detecting Logic for Digital Computers." McGraw-Hill, New York, 1968.

71. W. C. Carter and P. R. Schneider, Design of dynamically checked computers. *In* "Information Processing 68" (A. J. H. Morrell, ed.), pp. 878–883. North-Holland Publ., Amsterdam, 1969.

72. J. von Neumann, Probabilistic logics and synthesis of reliable organisms from unreliable components, *Automata Studies (Ann. Math. Studies No. 34),* pp. 43–98. Princeton Univ. Press, Princeton, New Jersey, 1956.

73. M. M. Dickinson, J. B. Jackson, and G. C. Rands, Saturn V launch vehicle digital computer and data adapter. *Proc. AFIPS Fall Joint Comput. Conf., 1964,* **26.** Spartan, Washington, D.C., 1964.

74. R. E. Kuehn, Computer redundance: Design, performance, and future. *IEEE Trans. Reliability* **R-18,** 3–11 (1969).

75. E. G. Andrews, The Bell computer, model VI. *Ann. Harvard Comput. Lab., Proc. Int. Symp. on Large Scale Digital Mach., 2nd, Cambridge, Massachusetts, September 13–16, 1949,* pp. 20–31. Harvard Univ. Press, Cambridge, Massachusetts, 1951.

76. M. Y. Hsiao and J. T. Tou, Application of error-correcting codes in computer reliability studies. *IEEE Trans. Reliability* **R-18,** 108–118 (1969).

77. R. A. Short, The attainment of reliable digital systems through the use of redundancy. *Comput. Group News* **2** (2), 2–17 (1968).

78. A. Avizienis, Design of fault-tolerant computers. *Proc. AFIPS Fall Joint Comput. Conf., 1967,* **31,** pp. 733–743. Thompson, Washington, D.C., 1967.

79. H. Y. Chang, E. G. Manning, and G. Metze, "Fault Diagnosis of Digital Systems." Wiley, New York, 1970.

80. D. J. Wheeler and J. E. Robertson, Diagnostic programs for the Illiac. *Proc. IRE* **41,** 1320–1325 (1953).

81. R. K. Richards, "Arithmetic Operations in Digital Computers." Van Nostrand-Reinhold, Princeton, New Jersey, 1955.

82. A. M. Johnson, Jr., Microprogram diagnostics for control storage processors. MSEE Thesis, Dept. of Elec. Eng., Syracuse Univ., Syracuse, New York, 1970.

83. A. M. Johnson, Jr., The microdiagnostics for the system/360 model 30. Tech. Rep. TR 01.1263. IBM Lab., Endicott, New York, July 30, 1970. (Presented at the *Annu. Workshop on Microprogramming, 3rd, Buffalo, New York, October 12–13, 1970.*)

84. R. Eldred, Test routines based on symbolic logical statements. *J. Assoc. Comput. Mach.* **6,** 33–36 (1959).

85. W. C. Carter, H. C. Montgomery, R. J. Preiss, and H. J. Reinheimer, Design of serviceability features for the IBM system/360. *IBM J. Res. Develop.* **8,** 115–126 (1964).

86. F. J. Hackl and R. W. Shirk, An integrated approach to automated computer maintenance. *Annu. Symp. Switching Circuit Theory and Logical Design, 6th, Ann Arbor, Michigan, October 1965,* IEEE Publ. **16 C13,** pp. 289–302.

87. J. Dent, Diagnostic engineering. *IEEE Spectrum* **4** (7), 99–104 (1967).

88. E. R. Jones and C. H. Mays, Automatic test generation methods for large scale integrated logic. *IEEE J. Solid-State Circuits* **SC-2,** 221–226 (1967).

89. P. R. Low, How IBM deals with the interface problem. "LSI: The Changing Interface," pp. 75–80. McGraw-Hill, New York, 1969.

90. W. Dunn, The testing interface. "LSI: The Changing Interface," pp. 59–63. McGraw-Hill, New York, 1969.
91. J. P. Roth, Diagnosis of automata failures: A calculus and a method. *IBM J. Res. Develop* **10**, 279–291 (1966).
92. G. G. Langdon, Jr. and C. K. Tang, Concurrent error detection for group look-ahead binary adders. *IBM J. Res. Develop.* **14** (5), 563–573 (1970).
93. J. P. Roth, W. G. Bouricius, and P. R. Schneider, Programmed algorithms to compute test to detect and distinguish between failures in logic circuits. *IEEE Trans. Comput.* EC-16, 567–580 (1967).
94. W. G. Bouricius, W. C. Carter, K. A. Duke, J. P. Roth, and P. R. Schneider, Interactive design of self-testing circuitry. Res. Rep. RC2444. IBM, Yorktown Heights, New York, April 18, 1969.
95. M. Y. Hsiao and D. K. Chia, Boolean difference for automatic test-pattern generation. *IEEE Trans. Comput.* C-20, 1356–1361 (1971).
96. J. F. Poage and E. J. McCluskey, Derivation of optimal test sequences for sequential machines. *Proc. Annu. Symp. Switching Theory and Logical Design, 5th, Princeton, New Jersey, October 1964,* IEEE Publ. S-164, pp. 121–132.
97. F. C. Hennie, Fault detection experiments in sequential circuits. *Proc. Annu. Symp. Switching Theory and Logical Design, 5th, Princeton, New Jersey, October 1964,* IEEE Publ. S-164, pp. 95–110.
98. M. Williams and J. Angell, Enhancing testability of large-scale integrated circuits via test points and additional logic. *IEEE Trans. Comput.* C-22, 46–60 (1973).
99. J. P. Roth, Design of automata, theory of cubical complexes with applications to diagnosis and algorithmic description. Tech. Rep. RC 3814. IBM Res., Yorktown Heights, New York, April 11, 1972.
100. A. D. Friedman and P. R. Menon, "Fault Detection in Digital Circuits." Prentice-Hall, Englewood Cliffs, New Jersey, 1971.
101. M. Kloomok, P. W. Case, and H. H. Graff, The recording, checking and printing of logic diagrams. *Proc. AFIPS Eastern Joint Comput. Conf., Philadelphia, Pennsylvania, December 1958,* **14**, pp. 108–118.
102. S. P. Krosher and W. H. Sass, Revisiting an operational graphic design system. *Proc. Annu. Design Automation Workshop, 8th, Atlantic City, New Jersey, 1971,* pp. 109–113. ACM, New York, 1971.
103. M. A. Breuer, ed.,"Design Automation of Digital Systems," Vol. 1. Prentice-Hall, Englewood Cliffs, New Jersey, 1972.
104. M. A. Breuer, Recent developments in the automated design and analysis of digital systems. *Proc. IEEE* **60**, 12–27 (1972).
105. S. S. Husson, "Microprogramming: Principles and Practices." Prentice-Hall, Englewood Cliffs, New Jersey, 1970.
106. W. H. Ware, "Digital Computer Technology and Design," Vol. II. Wiley, New York, 1963.
107. C. L. Wanlass, Transistor circuitry for digital computers. *IRE Trans. Electron. Comput.* EC-4, 11–15 (1955).
108. J. Earle, Logic and timing in digital system design. *Electron. Design* 8 (16), 30–42 (1961).
109. J. C. Sims, Jr. and H. J. Gray, Design criteria for autosynchronous circuits, *Proc. AFIPS Eastern Comput. Conf., Philadelphia, Pennsylvania, December 1958,* **14**, pp. 94–99.
110. J. R. Smith, Jr. and C. H. Roth, Jr., Differential mode analysis and synthesis of sequential switching networks. Clearinghouse Rep. AD-697 189, March 1969, NTIS, Springfield, Virginia 22151; see also *IEEE Trans. Comput.* C-20, 847–855 (1971).

111. G. A. Maley, "Manual of Logic Circuits." Prentice-Hall, Englewood Cliffs, New Jersey, 1970.
112. E. L. Braun, "Digital Computer Design." Academic Press, New York, 1963.
113. H. J. Gray, "Digital Computer Engineering." Prentice-Hall, Englewood Cliffs, New Jersey, 1963.
114. J. B. Peatman, "The Design of Digital Systems." McGraw-Hill, New York, 1972.

Chapter 4

Interrelationships

In the first three chapters we have concentrated primarily on three topics: the technology, sequential machine theory, and the logic design of computers. In this chapter we concentrate on the interrelationships. We view the relative strengths of the relationships as being those depicted in Fig. 4.1. The technology, due to its importance with respect to system cost, holds the most important relationship to logic design. Switching theory is less strongly related to logic design and has an even weaker relationship with digital system design as a whole. We also give particular attention to the interaction between theory and practice. Elspas [1] has stated that "developments, in which practice outstrips the theory, are not uncommon in technology"; this is the case in computer design. This chapter seeks to uncover causes for the disparity and suggests ways to improve the relationship.

A. Technology and Logic Design

In teaching computer design there is a tendency to treat the logic gates as "black boxes." For example, Foster states that the logic designer is not concerned with how his gates are made or what transistors (if any) they use[2]. However, the designer must know how the gates behave. Professor C. Gordon Bell points out: "Real design occurs with real components and much that makes design an intellectual challenge derives from the fact that only certain particular components are available out of all possible

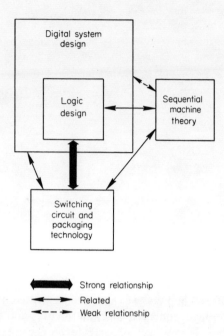

Fig. 4.1. Relationship of digital system design to switching circuit technology, sequential machine theory, and logic design.

components." † He feels "absolute familiarity with the components available contributes substantially to the ability to design." † Professor Bell is correct because knowledge of not only the components but the constraints of the packaging scheme can expose favorable trade-offs which can be used to reduce the system cost. It is the cost factor that distinguishes engineering from science, and the logic designer is an engineer. Today a major contributor to the system hardware cost is in the packaging. This fact is reflected in a book by Kohonen [4] where he treated on equal footing the standard logic design topics found in most texts, and aspects of its hardware implementation. The failure on the part of many people to appreciate the role of technology and packaging is illustrated by the reaction in an *IEEE Transactions on Computers* review of Kohonen's book. It questioned the wisdom of this "equal footing," stating that many other topics (such as programming) were related to logic design. In fact, knowledge of no other topic (including programming) is capable of helping the logic designer as much in reducing the cost of his design.

† From C. G. Bell, J. Grason, and A. Newell [3], "Designing Computers and Digital Systems." © 1972, Digital Press, Maynard, Massachusetts. Reprinted by permission.

In evolving new technologies, the logic designer, circuit technologist, and solid-state technologist may interact. The circuit and device engineers are interested in providing useful products to the logic designer, and in turn, the logic designer is interested in making his preferences known.

A necessary ingredient for the construction of a digital system is what Braun called a system of circuit logic, i.e., a family of logic circuits. The relationship between the logic designer and his circuit family is particularly strong since he must account for meeting the fan-in and fan-out constraints, the wiring rules, and the worst-case delay paths within the data flow.

Knowledge of the circuitry is important to the system designer in the selection of a technology with which to build a specific digital system. The choice may depend on the cost, power, noise, reliability, density, and/or speed requirements of the system, and it will influence the selection of meeting these requirements with some current technology such as C-MOS (Complementary Metal–Oxide Semiconductor) or TTL (Transistor–Transistor Logic).

B. Technology and Switching Theory

The technology preceded the design of digital systems, digital system design preceded theory, and the mathematical models were drawn from the technology. The technology is characterized by variety; and as such, a large variety of logic and timing schemes have resulted. Consequently, a knowledge of the technology is a key to understanding a cause of the gap between theory and practice.

Many textbooks caution the reader on the "subtle" differences between the Moore and Mealy models; however, the real difference is in the technology: Mealy and Moore were motivated by different physical memory elements. The difference is between the pulse-output SEAC dynamic flip-flop and the level-output Eccles–Jordan flip-flop. The difficulty of making simplifying assumptions and abstracting "universal models" is exemplified by the Whirlwind I level-output flip-flops; here the logic designer could generate pulse outputs that he needed by combining level signals with a pulse in a gated pulse amplifier. This memory element, having pulse output and not unit delay feedback, fits neither the Moore nor Mealy models. The idiosyncrasies of the memory elements do not invalidate the notion of the sequential machine next-state function, and the models stand as valuable conceptual entities. The author believes that the model merely supplements the logic designer's knowledge of the technology and does not supplant it.

Pulsed techniques were obsoleted by the difficulty of making capacitors in bipolar integrated circuit technology; and yet, rigidly synchronized techniques exist today because of very inexpensive dynamic MOS FETs. The important consideration for a technology is its cost, and not the model it may realize, and technologies that do not offer a cost-competitive function become little more than a laboratory curiosity. LSI has interested designers since it has a low cost per circuit, relative to competing technologies. However, attendant LSI cost considerations are forcing designers to consider designs with fewer part numbers and fewer interconnections. The part number problem has motivated many theoretical studies on "universal logic elements" which comprise only one or two circuit types. Unfortunately, the approaches have all created solutions at the expense of more pins and increased wiring.

The theoretical methods developed for existing models assist in evaluating (and designing with) newer technologies which resemble earlier technologies. For example, had cryogenics become a viable technology, the existing body of knowledge on designing with relays could have been used. Some of the theoretical minimization methods have been adapted to accommodate varying cost criteria.

This writer's feeling is that for the field of engineering the theory ought to be adapted to the technology and not the other way around. For example, attempts to "force" threshold logic elements out of primarily binary devices have not been successful. In a theoretical study of transition-sensitive flip-flops published in the *IEEE Transactions on Computers,* a circuit that performed a function much more complicated (and only slightly more useful) than the three-device differential of Fig. 1.6 cost eight transistors, 21 diodes, 17 resistors, and two capacitors. Ideas that either demand too much from the technology, or which totally ignore cost considerations, are best valued and identified as scientific and intellectual contributions rather than as contributions to engineering.

C. Logic Design and Programming

Before discussing the relationship between switching theory and logic design, we wish to comment on computer programming. The relationship between programming and logic design, for a particular project, depends on the architectural phase (see Table 3.1). In projects involving a family of medium- to large-scale systems, the architecture may be defined relatively independently of particular logic design considerations and the realization of the design does not require a background in programming. If the design is to be microprogrammed, however, then the system designer utilizes both logic design and microprogramming techniques in the development process. In many small computer designs (say less than a few thousand gates), the architects, logic designers, and systems designers are probably a well-integrated group of people and familiarity with programming is necessary if the design is to implement a new architecture. (Often, however, the design may implement an existing architecture and the interaction with programming is less critical.)

A technological advance which is affecting the practice of logic design is the existence of the LSI microprocessor; a data flow and control on one to several LSI chips. In this case, the logic designers' building blocks are data flows, control stores, and read/write memory chips. He arranges the chips and programs the control store.

A design viewpoint and method intended for programming systems, called "iterative multilevel modeling," has been described by Zurcher and Randall [5]. The method incorporates simulating or modeling an evolving design as an integral part of the effort and acknowledges the existence of states of partial design. The technique is oriented to structuring the design process with the "top-down" or "outside-in" approach. For the "top-down" approach, the system is first viewed as a single entity, then divided into components, and then into subcomponents. The hierarchy structure of the model is in terms of *levels of abstraction.* This does *not* mean the system is viewed as a nested structure of black boxes within black boxes. The concept of levels of abstraction permits several representations of varying detail to coexist. At a lower (more detailed) level of abstraction, a signal line of communication or control may appear where at a higher level it does not. This point is observed by Parnas [6]; he states that the term "extent of functional decomposition" is reserved to describe the nested structure, where no new interconnections show up as the design progresses into greater detail.

The iterative multilevel concept might be very useful in logic design. Both programming and logic design are faced with the task of constructing complex systems out of small building blocks. The concept of levels of abstraction is therefore a valuable contribution toward a better understanding of the design process and may represent a promising direction toward more realistic design methods.

D. Logic Design and Switching Theory

In designing a code to protect information stored on magnetic tapes, coding theory is very useful. In designing a bipolar NOR or NAND gate, the model of the transistor, and the use of circuit theory is quite useful. In designing MOS logic circuits, the current–voltage relationship for the MOS field-effect transistor is of high relevance. In designing a digital system, however, switching theory, although used, does not play a correspondingly important role. In a book on digital systems design, Bell *et al.* do not include material on Boolean algebra and binary numbers. They explain in the preface, "Both concepts are not used in substantial quantities, although the reader may feel they are needed to thoroughly understand all of the problems." † In the preface to his book, Chu correctly comments on the application of sequential circuit theory to the logic design phase. He completely omitted sequential switching circuit theory because he felt the symbolic method to be more useful in handling sequential circuits [7].

Logic designers have long recognized that the most creative part (or perhaps, the least scientific part) of the design procedure is the "functional" or "strategic" phase; in this phase the system is viewed as a set of functional units connected by the data and control paths. Gorman has noted that beginning with a marketing specification and carrying it to a functional design is not a well-enough defined process to be handled by automation [8]. This may be due to the inadequacy of the sequential circuit model, as observed by Phister: "Furthermore, it does not of itself suggest a procedure for the logical designer to follow in translating a system description of a computer into a description in terms of this model. If it did, all designer's problems would be solved." ‡ The symbolic method is preferred over sequential machine methods because it conforms closer to the design process and system timing. In the IBM System/360 Model 50 (and in many other machines), the basic operation of a machine cycle consists of gating the contents of two source registers to the arithmetic unit inputs, performing an operation on the data while in the arithmetic unit, temporarily storing the result in the latches, and then gating the result back to a register. Thus, since the data flow is already designed and since the register transfers that take place for each machine cycle are described by micro-operations and implemented by combinational circuits, few applications remain for the Moore, Mealy, or fundamental mode models. The applications that are candidates for a theoretical approach include the cycle controls (I-cycles, E-cycles, etc.) and console controls (start, stop, run, halt, pause, single cycle, display memory, write memory, etc.).

---

† From C. G. Bell, J. Grason and A. Newell [3], "Designing Computers and Digital Systems." © 1972, Digital Press, Maynard, Massachusetts. Reprinted by permission.

‡ From M. Phister [9], "Logical Design of Digital Computers." © 1958, John Wiley & Sons, New York. Reprinted by permission.

1. The Timing of the Models

The use of a sequential machine model generally implies two things: the use of a particular timing scheme and a problem statement in the form of a flow table. In this section, the former implication is treated.

The Moore and Mealy models imply a single-phase clock, generally a pulse, whereas few system designers choose such a clock; the multiphased clock offers more flexibility. For the methods derived from Huffman's work, the timing is assumed to be unclocked. Very few systems today are unclocked. Runyan noted as early in 1959 that clocked circuits were easier to design than unclocked (asynchronous) ones, and that unclocked designs were "noted by their rarity" [10]. It occurred to Seshu, however, that fundamental mode operation could be used for his "Sequential Analyser" simulation program, when one treats the clock signals as primary inputs that change after the circuit has settled from the previous change [11]. This type of operation has been called clocked fundamental mode. Maley and Earle imply this type of operation when they say most computers are synchronous systems designed from asynchronous sequential elements and that clock pulses are used to give the effect of inserted delay [12]. Unfortunately, this statement is not clear. It means most systems have a central clock, that level-sensitive combinational circuits and memory elements are used, and that the clock is multiphased so the logic designer can use the different phases to allow for worst-case delays in combinational circuits and thus avoid critical races. In the theoretical literature, however, clocked fundamental mode is not common. Not helping this situation is a comment in a widely used text that clocked fundamental mode is rarely used [13]. Loomis [14] in another context, however, has studied the timing relationships in a clocked environment that uses a two phase nonoverlapping clock signals, with level-sensitive polarity-hold (sample-and-hold) flip-flops. The primary objective of Loomis is to analyze a network of "clock pulse propagators" which generates the clock pulses. However, with the identification of the "clock width uncertainty" of Loomis with possible clock skew and "jitter" in a real system, the analysis holds. In a book by Husson [15] the timing of several machines is described. The systems use multiphase clocks and many use level-sensitive memory elements. Actually, the wide use of clock pulses with fundamental mode circuits should not come as a surprise. The fundamental mode assumption implies that the "environment" does not change the inputs until the circuit has reached a stable condition. One may ask how the environment is expected to know the circuit has attained a stable condition? Very few theoretical investigations provide for a completion signal; rather mention is made of an upper bound on circuit delays. Again, the question may be asked: how does the environment know this upper bound on delays has expired so that the inputs may be changed? Many investigations have not addressed this question. This same situation exists in practice; however, it is solved because a multi-phase clock is generally available and worst-case delays are accounted for by appropriate use of the timing signals. The result is the clocked funda-mental mode.

2. The Large Number of Inputs in Real Designs

One problem in applying the theory arises where a functional unit (or any section of logic) involves a large number of input signals. With regard to designing control circuits, Richards [16] comments that although Boolean algebra is a useful tool, it is inadequate when applied to the multi-plicity of signals encountered. In a more recent book, Richards [17] again mentions the large number of variables in practical systems and the existence of "messy" complicating factors which defeat the application of theoretical techniques to other than well-defined problems.

Why is there a large number of variables with which to deal? Perhaps "Rent's curve" can provide a clue. Rent made a study in 1960 and con-cluded that to partition manually a large amount of logic into packages of c circuits, the pin count is given by Ac^P, where $P = \frac{2}{3}$ and A is a constant [18]. Rent discovered that the IBM 1401 had a constant A of 4.8; however, depending on the average gate fan-in for a design, the constant A could vary from 3 to 5 [19]. The empirical curve applies to designs where no spe-cial effort has been made to reduce interconnections. In any case, if one assumed a circuit composed of 25 gates, then about 20 input–output signals could be expected for a conventional design. If one assumed that 10 of these were input signals, then the Huffman flow table would contain 1024 columns! To appreciate this point, the reader is invited to look at some logic diagrams from the maintenance documents of any machine, and count the number of flip-flops and the number of input signal lines on some pages selected at random. A previously stated advantage of the flow table is that it forces the designer to consider all input conditions. However, this is no longer advantageous if the flow table becomes so large that the ap-proach is discarded.

Invariably, some input signals have more "significance" than others; for example, some inputs may be clocking signals and others may be reset signals whose treatment can be postponed until after the basic circuit has been designed. This technique is employed by Maley and Earle [12]; i.e., they have designed basic circuits, such as triggers, by using flow table tech-niques, and later they have determined where the reset signal could be ap-plied. The functional unit then can be viewed as performing some functions or operations "most of the time." After the circuits that perform these major operations are designed, the design is then modified to handle the "messy" complicating factors. This approach, called the interactive approach, is widely used in practice—however, not always because the designer set out to do it that way. (The mark of an experienced logic designer is the ability to modify a design to meet a new contingency or to remove a known bug with a minimum of effort.)

3. The Flow Table as a Point of Departure for Design

Theoretical methods use the flow table as the starting point of a design. This feature ought not obscure the fact that sequential circuits are meant to realize digital systems, and not flow tables, and designers prefer methods where they can keep this end result in mind.

Although a sequential circuit may have many input states, it does not need to have hundreds of internal states. Therefore, although a flow table may become unwieldy, a state transition graph need not. Further, a state transition graph is more easily understood. An important contribution to the adaptation of theory to practice was made by Schultz [20]; he draws upon the designer's basic understanding of the problem and requires him to identify the "infrequent variables." Loosely defined, these variables do not relate to all internal states, i.e., they are not needed to define every state. In essence, the infrequent variables are relevant to only a few (perhaps one or two) states or state transitions. Schultz suggests that the designer first translate the verbal problem to a state transition graph that is reduced. The internal states are encoded and then information regarding infrequent variables is added to the appropriate state transitions. A "first approximation" to flip-flop input equations is made, based only upon the frequent variables. Schultz demonstrates how these equations can subsequently be modified to incorporate transitions controlled by the infrequent variables. In Schultz's examples the infrequent variables are all input signals, but this idea also applies to internal state variable signals that may be considered "infrequent." In this case, for example, an infrequent internal state variable flip-flop might be set by a particular circumstance and reset sometime later. The output of the flip-flop may now be treated as an infrequent input variable.

Bentley [21] also avoids the flow table description, choosing the flow chart description and then rearranging the flow chart to make it appear as a state transition graph. He uses clocked JK flip-flops, synchronized by a single clock pulse.

4. The Changing Circuit Specifications

Further complications with the application of sequential theory arise because the initial definition of the functional units will most often be imprecise; i.e., although a designer will have a general idea of the operations to be performed by each functional unit, he cannot obtain the exact specification of the signals that interface with functional units. Even if a precise functional specification did exist, it would be subject to change due to implementation considerations (e.g., excessive cost, too many levels of gate delays, or a deficiency of signal pins at some packaging level). These changes made to the logic are called *engineering changes*.

Bell [3] notes that digital systems design is an "open activity." The design specifications in many cases are "loose," particularly in minicomputer or microcomputer design where the logic designer provides the maximum function he can obtain under the constraints imposed such as a power or package boundary (limitation). The detailed design phase may be in a continual state of flux as the design is modified. In many cases the specifications may change in order to minimize circuits. Combinational circuit minimization procedures apply to a fixed problem specification. Suppose a microinstruction has a three-bit field, each of whose eight combinations are intended to perform a diversity of micro-operations to control an arithmetic unit. For some combinations, certain micro-operations may be in common. Is there a way to assign combinations to micro-operations which minimizes the control logic? Once combinations are assigned, the problem is to design a multiple-output combinational circuit. This can be described by a truth table, and theoretical methods apply. The assigning of the combinations, however, is analogous to changing the columns and rows of the truth table, in short, to changing the problem specification. This is but an example of the freedom a logic designer may have in changing circuit specifications.

Machart has said, "The process of obtaining pertinent system design information is always the most difficult, tedious, and treacherous portion of any design problem. Very few feasibility projects have all input and output signals precisely defined, nor do they even remain static through system design and debug procedures. Thus, classical optimal methods, although powerful in a static world, have little practical value in a changing environment" [22]. Unfortunately, sequential machine synthesis techniques are relevant only once the major problem, obtaining a precise definition, has been solved.

Machart has attacked the general logic design problem in a "changing environment." The procedure is exemplified by means of a simplified control unit design problem. The control unit operation is explained, some assumptions stated, a data flow is drawn up, and a timing sequence chart is presented. From this information a system flow chart is constructed. Machart's next step is to convert the flow chart into a state transition graph. Branches or system states of the flow chart become nodes on the graph. Machart observes that timing information (i.e., the signal from the central clock which is AND gated with the control signals) may be included here rather than at the flow chart level. Machart assumed a four-phase clock existed for his example, and he resolved state transition timings and gated output pulses with an appropriate phase from the clock. (This portion of the design is not readily described by an algorithm.) In his four-state example, he utilized one flip-flop per state. Machart argues that encoding the states may reduce the number of flip-flops required; however, more complicated flip-flop input equations result.

The control unit receives commands from a master device. The master may pass commands to the control unit, or it may reset the control unit. The control unit interfaces with a servant device to which it passes the commands. The servant device may be busy or not busy, and will indicate if data are ready. Data transfer is from the servant to the master, the control unit indicates data are stable by signal "Service Request" and the master indicates it has received it by the signal "Service Response." The state transition graph is shown in Fig. 4.2. The realization procedure specifies a set-clear flip-flop for each of states a, b, c, and d; the set and clear conditions for each are evident for Fig. 4.2, for example, flip-flop c is set by (a $T2 \cdot$ COMMAND NOT BUSY) and is reset by (RESET $+ b + d$). This design problem also illustrates the unwieldly characteristic of the flow table. The control unit has six primary control inputs plus four clock inputs, the flow table would have 512 columns. Even discarding the clock

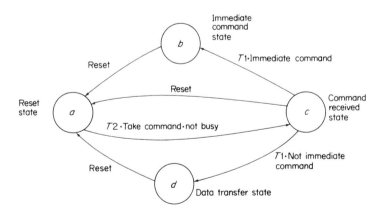

Fig. 4.2. A simple control unit problem. *Outputs:* $c \cdot T3$: set BUSY; $d \cdot T3$ DATA READY: set SERVICE REQUEST; $d \cdot$ SERVICE RESPONSE $\cdot T4$: reset SERVICE REQUEST, reset DATA READY.

inputs, the flow table would have 32 columns. The state transition graph is more intuitive, provides an understanding of the problem, and is simpler to use.

As a result of a change in the design specification for a "minimum flip-flop" design, the state reduction and state assignment procedures would have to be repeated; however, in the design of one flip-flop per state, a new state can be incorporated by little more than adding proper set–reset conditions. (Also note that excessive state encoding to reduce the number of state variables obscures what is going on and makes it difficult for maintenance people to understand the design.) Machart states that once the state diagram and timing is worked out, the bulk of the design phase is completed. The "mop-up" phase involving decode logic, clocking, line drivers, and line receivers is relatively straightforward. The use of the clock signals was fairly arbitrary, and this is a parameter the designer can vary.

5. Design Habits

Bell [3] has commented that the design process involves bridging the large gap between the design specifications and the given components. He states that in order to jump the gap, one creates subsystems which perform intermediate-sized tasks. Bell *et al.* [3] compare this process to the game of chess. The chess master, through experience, can recognize a large number of specific intermediate situations, and this is more useful than knowing general strategies. Similarly, for logic design, there is no substitute for acquiring knowledge of many partial solutions, and this can be gained only by immersing oneself in the design experience.

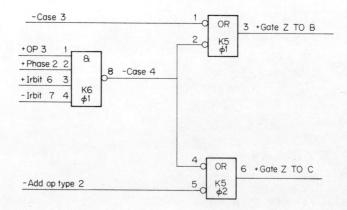

Fig. 4.3. A simple example of a section of control logic.

An important part of the design process is the debugging phase, and this teaches one to think about logic in a different way. The designers generally use logic drawings for the circuit description. If debugging is done on the hardware, these drawings also provide packaging information (pins, package locations, etc.) to assist in placing an oscilloscope on certain signal lines. The debugging phase is an intensive period where the designer becomes very familiar with the logic. The designer acquires the habit of seeing the drawing and visualizing what it does, independent of a truth table or flow table. Figure 4.3 depicts a simple example of some control logic. This example illustrates some mundane aspects of real design. A signal name, such as "CASE 3," indicates a condition. The minus sign before the name means that when the signal is at "low" voltage, then CASE 3 exists. Similarly, a signal called +CASE 3 implies the existence (or "assertion") of CASE 3 when the signal is at "high" voltage. In the examples that follow, *high* and *low* will be used to describe the possible states of a signal line. In Fig. 4.3, either CASE 3 or CASE 4 cause the Z Register to be gated to the B Register. The signal CASE 4 is generated by four-input NAND gate K6-01. Gate K5-01 is also a NAND, but is "behaving" as an OR of signals CASE 3 and CASE 4 hence is depicted as shown to reflect that behavior. The popular TTL (Transistor–Transistor Logic) family basically performs NAND logic. A NAND gate performs the AND function of the high (+) input states but delivers a low (−) output. It may also be viewed as performing an OR on low (−) inputs and then delivering a high (+) output.

For the other circuit output, either CASE 4 or ADD OR TYPE 2 cause

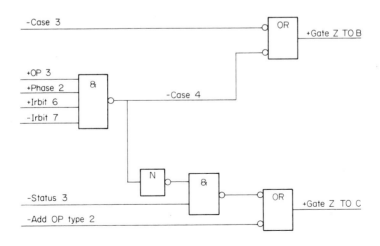

Fig. 4.4. A correction to a simple control circuit.

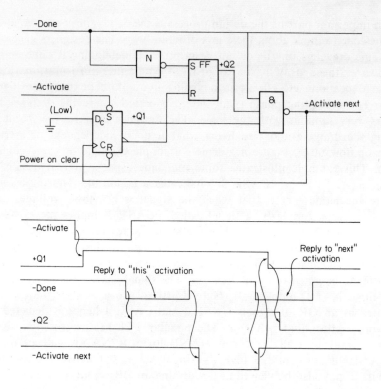

Fig. 4.5. A sequential circuit, K (evoke), of the PDP-16 RTL module series.

the Z Register to be gated to Register C. Suppose due to a bug one wanted to inhibit the gating of the C Register for CASE 4 if a signal called STATUS 3 were valid. This could be done by adding a five-input NAND with the appropriate inputs, and connecting the output to input 4 of gate "K5-02." Alternatively, the method of Fig. 4.4 can be employed, where signal CASE 4 is inhibited from activiting GATE Z to C by STATUS 3. This method does not increase the loading of the signals feeding gate K6-01, but it inserts two more gate delays in the path of signal GATE Z to C. This method also does not require a five-input NAND, which may not be readily available. In large part, many of the combinational circuits found in digital computers are not unlike this example; in themselves relatively simple "AND–OR" type logic with concern for fan-in and delays.

In another example, a simple sequential circuit is described. The circuit and its timing chart appears in Fig. 4.5. It is a slightly redrawn version of the K (evoke) circuit for the PDP-16 register transfer module set [3]. Several of these circuits are connected in series to control a sequence of register transfers. The first flip-flop $Q1$ is an edge-sensitive D, which changes on the positive-going edge of the signal at input C. The second flip-flop $Q2$ is a level-sensitive "set-clear" flip-flop. The circuit operates as follows, the signal $-DONE$ connects to all K (evoke) circuits. It is the result of all completion signals OR gated together. POWER ON CLEAR initializes the edge-sensitive D flip-flop $Q1$ to the clear state. This also clears the set-clear flip-flop $Q2$. A purpose of this example is to acquaint the reader with how logic designers view sequential logic.

When $-ACTIVATE$ goes low, i.e., is asserted, flip-flop $Q1$ is "set." Signal $-ACTIVATE$, causes some register transfer or micro-operation to be performed, at the completion of which $-DONE$ goes low. This causes the signal $-ACTIVATE$ (which comes from the previous K (evoke)) to return to high, it also sets flip-flop $Q2$. Subsequently, $-DONE$ will return high. This will cause $-ACTIVATE$ NEXT to go low, causing the next K (evoke) to perform some micro-operation. When the next micro-operation is completed, $-DONE$ will again go low, causing $-ACTIVATE$ NEXT to go high. This "edge" clears the edge-sensitive D flip-flop $Q1$. This in turn clears flip-flop $Q2$. The K (evoke) circuit now waits for its next activation.

With the above explanation, a logic designer can visualize the drawing of Fig. 4.5, understand how it operates, and if necessary, modify it. This circuit was redesigned by Bell *et al.* [3] using fundamental mode techniques. Two internal state variables Y0 and Y1 are used. A slightly redrawn version of their result appears in Fig. 4.6, along with a timing chart. The internal states differ from Fig. 4.5. The behavioral description of this circuit possesses an essential hazard, and the double inverters 7 and 8 following signal Y0 are intended to provided some delay. POWER ON CLEAR, when asserted, clears Y0 and Y1. At (1) on the timing chart, when ACTIVATE is asserted ($-ACTIVATE$ goes low), $+Y0$ goes high. Were $+Y0$ to go high at the OR gate before it "sees" $-ACTIVATE$ go low, a "glitch" may pass through the OR gate resulting in $+Y1$ erroneously being asserted. The double inverter delay provides security against this malfunction. Another hazard (the only one mentioned in Bell *et al.* [3]) is a critical race which exists at (2) of the timing chart. Here, $+Y1$ goes high causing Y0 to go low. Signal $+Y1$ should feed back to cause gate 2 to switch before the $+Y0$ change feeds back to gate 1. This problem is not too critical, as the $+Y1$ change must propagate through gates 6, 5, and 4 (in that order) before gate 1 can be influenced.

The circuit of Fig. 4.6 can be redrawn to display the secondary variables Y0 and Y1 as flip-flop outputs. When this is done, it is noticed that the output of gate 2 is always the complement of $+Y1$, hence inverter 6 is unnecessary. Further, if one assumes a line (interconnection) delay always wins a race against a gate delay (and its attendant line delays), then in-

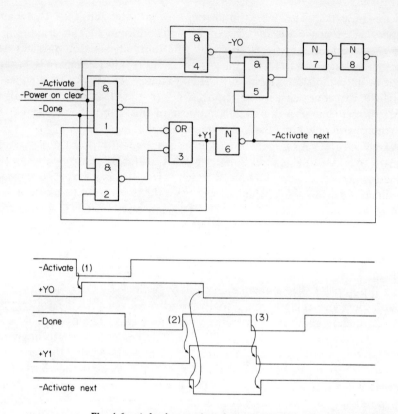

Fig. 4.6. A fundamental mode version of Fig. 4.5.

verters 7 and 8 are not needed. The new circuit appears in Fig. 4.7. (If additional protection against the hazard of transition (1) of Fig. 4.6 is needed, then the output of gate 5 can be inverted and fed to gate 1, instead of using $+Y0$.)

This example provides the background for several comments. First, the essential hazard problem for the circuit of Fig. 4.5 is avoided by the use of the edge-sensitive D flip-flop. Unfortunately, there are as yet no synthesis procedures for exploiting the edge-sensitive D flip-flop as was done here. Second, this writer feels the logic diagram of Fig. 4.5 is more easily understood, since the flip-flop controls (set and clear signals) are simpler. Since logic designers use logic diagrams as the basic design document, they acquire the habit of thinking in these terms. A circuit that is more easily understood (hence, more easily modified) is preferable during the design phase than one where the circuit behavior is obscured. Often the designers then do not have the time or inclination to risk modifying a circuit known to work in order to save a few gates.

We also note that the circuit of Fig. 4.5 has a different internal state structure than the circuit of Fig. 4.6. The circuits are behaviorally equivalent; the structural differences stem in part from the use of different memory elements. Today the designer is seen to have some control over the circuit component selection.

A final point concerns the fact that the theory only provides the boolean statements for variables $Y0$ and $Y1$. The manipulations to go from the circuit of Fig. 4.6 to that of Fig. 4.7 are based on the designers intuition, and ability to visualize how the blocks behave. It was most probably the method of trial and error with a logic diagram, coupled with experience, which gave rise to the circuit of Fig. 4.5.

E. Theory versus Practice

Two general academic fields are connected with the computer professions. The first, historically, is the design and manufacture of these tools, and the second is the application of the tool to the many problems

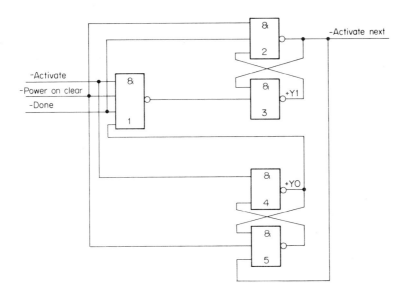

Fig. 4.7. A redesigned fundamental mode version of Fig. 4.5.

that require computation. The first field is loosely called computer engineering, computer design, or digital system design, and the second is now being called computer science. The theory versus practice problems of these fields have some similarities. Hamming spoke on his views of emphasizing the use of engineering in the second field, computer science [23]. He characterized science as dealing with what is possible and engineering as dealing with choosing the most economical and most practical solution from many possible approaches. In other words, engineering deals with "trade-offs," and cost plays an important role.

Richards has pointed out that the published technical papers in digital systems fall into two distinct categories: theory or practice; he notes that the relationship between them is not close. In 1968, Stanford Research Institute (SRI) formed a workshop composed of about a dozen SRI researchers and university professors to study this relationship. The introduction to their report states: "there seems to be a greater gap between the theory of logical systems and its corresponding practical arts than between the theory and arts of other engineering disciplines," and that "there is a general feeling that the gap between theory and practice is growing" [1].

1. Experience and the Communication Gap

The practicing engineer and the theorist often do not speak the same language, and often do not read the same literature. This lack of communication is called the communication gap, and a symptom of this gap is that one side feels the "other" side uses excessive jargon. The reader can test his own prejudice by picking from the following terms the ones that make him uncomfortable: *wired-or, lift-set* and *drop-set, minterm, dual in-line package, p-cube, maximal compatible, glitch, jam transfer, disjunctive element, unicode STT assignments, inverter.* (Note that all of these items are known and accepted within their field.)

Many practitioners feel that much theoretical work lacks relevance since many researchers lack practical experience. Phister points out in his book that no one can become a logic designer by studying books, there being no substitute for experience [9]. A similar feeling is expressed by Hamming regarding computer science: "without real experience in using the computer to get useful results, the computer science major is apt to know all about the marvelous tool except how to use it."†

The logic designers who debated at the 1958 Western Joint Computer Conference made the point that logic design is an art. Logic designers are

---

† From R. W. Hamming [23], One Man's View of Computer Science, *J. ACM* **16** (1), pp. 3–12, © January 1969, Association for Computing Machinery. Reprinted by permission.

rarely inclined to solicit the advice or opinion of others outside their design group and are even less inclined to listen to those with no machine experience. Unless one does some logic design, the author feels he will lack something—perhaps a particular attitude or measure of appreciation—that familiarity with the technical literature cannot supply. A difference in attitude is exemplified by today's viewpoint toward synthesis. Researchers treat synthesis as the realization of some abstract sequential circuit model such as the Huffman or Mealy model; whereas, to a logic designer, synthesis is used to organize the physical circuits to realize the behavioral description of the functional unit.

The technical literature should and sometimes does serve as a bridge across the communication gap between the theorist and practitioner. But the theoretical literature is read by few practicing engineers, and trade magazines are not widely read by theorists. Part of the problem is the use of overly esoteric terminology. The inadequacy of the terms *synchronous* and *asynchronous* has already been discussed; another case in point is the needless and confusing use of terms such as *acyclic* where *combinational* is meant. Bad terminology does not enhance the communication process or rapport between the researcher and the engineer. Elspas [1] attributes part of the communication gap to theorists who are not "popularizers" of their field. Perhaps the same situation exists with logic designers, many of whom are reluctant to write articles even if they had the time to write.

Sometimes when reading a work in the technical literature, one gets the feeling of a make believe atmosphere. It is almost as if the technology and design experience of the first generation gave rise to a body of literature (much of the basis of which appears in a textbook by Caldwell [24]), and that many researchers and textbook writers interacted more with that body of literature than with actual design experience. One problem facing an engineer who wants to learn more about theory is the large quantity of books of varying quality. (In fact, within a single book the quality between chapters may vary widely.) To be aware of all these books is very difficult, and quite obviously, some outstanding chapters may go largely unappreciated. Textbooks on switching theory could serve as a better bridge between theory and practice by indicating the applicability of the theory and describing common engineering practices. The idea that a logic designer divides his machine into Huffman flow tables and then applies synthesis procedures contradicts the facts, but unfortunately many texts on switching theory fail to bring this out. Often the pulse mode model described by Caldwell [24] receives considerable attention in texts and the clocked fundamental mode receives barely any, whereas over the last decade the former mode is almost nonexistant and the latter almost predominates.

2. Role of Universities

The universities educate many of the computer designers and are thus in a unique position to influence practice. For computer science, Hamming recommends a stiff laboratory course to provide experience in "true-to-life" programming [23]. The same recommendation applies to logic design. In this case, it is even adequate to simulate the hardware on another computer [25] although the advent of the minicomputer has placed hardware within the reach of most universities [26]. A laboratory involving a technology such as TTL would be useful. Another recommendation would be to have post doctoral graduates who intend to teach in the computer field spend a few years getting practical experience. A problem of computer science that was brought out at the 1970 Fall Joint Computer Conference was that almost all computer science Ph.Ds went into staffing other computer science departments, which causes an inbreeding of theory [27]. At a meeting of the ACM Special Interest Group on Computer Science Education, Robert R. Korfhage of Southern Methodist University made some excellent points. He suggested the business world develop exchange programs with universities. He also suggested that professors take on consulting work as a means to receive stimulus from the real world. Universities train two groups of students: those who will enter practice, and those who will enter research or teaching. However, the university should not train one group to the exclusion of the other. Instructors of courses in computer design would do well to follow the systematic approach advocated by Chu. Digital engineers whose education does not include an exposure to a systematic procedure based on micro-operations, often turn to an unsystematic "cut-and-try" approach for logic design. Further, technological considerations should be stressed.

Much of the early impetus to the computer field was provided by universities. Today, many universities have projects in applied research, particularly in the areas of computer architecture, data organization, information retrieval, programming systems, hierarchical structure, and computer systems evaluation. Theory and practice had a much closer relationship in the first generation; this was a result of the practice performed at universities, where the technology and design practices of that generation were in large part developed. Today, many universities are providing excellent training to students through the use of minicomputers and microcomputers. The minicomputer serves not only as a valuable teaching aid, but also provides master's thesis topics for the students who design the peripheral equipment interfaces.

Some universities have hardware design programs; historically the University of Illinois has been most active in this area. Washington

University has developed some interesting concepts with their "macromodular" approach [28]. A result of this practical work led to the discovery of a possible "glitch" in circuits which synchronize incoming signals to a clocked system [29], this phenomenon was commented on in a widely read scientific magazine [30]. At Carnegie-Mellon University, register transfer modules (RTL) were devised which are now marketed by DEC [3]. These latter developments may represent a revival of interest in the job completion signal approach.

3. The Theory Pursued as Pure and Not Applied Research

Up to this point, this chapter has dealt with the art of logic design from a practical viewpoint. Having shown that digital system design has motivated considerable theoretical research, need the researcher apologize if his work is of no practical value? The author thinks he need not. The ancient Greeks apologized to no one for their discourse on topics that had no immediate practical application. The Greeks made estimates of the distance of the earth from the sun and of the diameter of the earth. These measurements may have been motivated by their interest in astrology, but they had no practical bearing on the art. Many problems are worth solving for the sheer satisfaction of curiosity. Humans are natively inquisitive individuals who enjoy investigating and discovering. If the work is motivated by a practical problem, so much the better, but why make practicality a requirement? On the other hand, the tendency for theorists to overemphasize the practical importance of the theory serves no useful purpose, and will mislead students.

Much work that appears in the literature will never have a practical application even though it was motivated by a real-world problem. For example, to imply that some day logic designers will apply a given state minimization technique in their work is pretentious; perhaps the communication gap appears wider than it really is because of this pretense. In order to foster an attitude of mutual respect between practitioners and applied researchers, the author feels researchers who wish to advance the state of the art should ensure they have an adequate practical background, and those more interested in science and theory for its own sake might pause and exercise some restraint before citing "practical applications" for their work. Here honesty is the best policy: Dr. Mow's comment on his dissertation on threshold logic concerned its possible usefulness 60 years after his death [31]. This should not be interpreted to mean that the work was a complete waste of time. Also, it should not imply that Mow's powers of reasoning did not benefit from the mental exercise required in stating a problem, analyzing it, providing a solution, and coherently transmitting that information to others. Einstein felt it of primary importance to master the fundamentals of a subject and to think and work independently, as opposed to the mere acquisition of specialized knowledge [32]. The pursuit of the theory as distinct from practice is thus useful to the individual on this basis, provided that its relation to practice is kept in proper perspective.

4. Simplifying Assumptions and Ad Hoc Procedures

In order to formulate a theory, one usually wishes to make simplifying assumptions and abstract the essentials from the technology so that the theory is not dependent upon the technology. This strategy can be carried too far, as Richards notes that the simplifying assumptions contained in published theoretical work may tend to move it away from the engineering world [17]. Thus it appears that a tractable mathematical theory can be constructed by many simplifying assumptions; whereas, the design of physical systems uses very few simplifying assumptions.

Viewing the large variety in logic and timing schemes, one may suspect that logic design practice is characterized by a large variety of techniques. Elspas says "there is a proliferation of ad hoc techniques, with varying degrees of mathematical content, developed for the cases at hand" [1]. The ad hoc methods provide competition to the theoretical ones. To compete with ad hoc procedures, theoretical methods must provide (1) a suitable model and (2) a result that is worth the effort. The more difficult the theory to understand or use, the correspondingly greater must be the result over ad hoc methods before it is adopted by engineers. Richards has stated that a design approach using a model convenient for theoretical treatment does not always yield a better result than the "cut-and-try" method [17]. When it comes to selecting design methods in practical designs, the methods are subject to cost versus performance trade-offs by the engineer; unless superior results are achieved from theoretical methods, they are not used.

F. Role of Theory

If all technical people were involved in the problems of development (i.e., cost, analysis, performance, practical design methods, and other engineering considerations), then little time would be left to reflect on broad theoretical questions. There is a need for work such as sorting out principles from intuition and discovering conditions under which certain techniques apply. Switching theory does not play a central role in computer design; however, its influence exists and is felt in many ways.

Although combinational switching theory was not reviewed in this work, it plays an important part in the language of the logic designer. The terms and concepts of this theory are taken for granted, and they provide a basis of communication between logic designers because they are independent of the technology. Boolean statements form a key tool in the Western school of logic design. Sequential switching theory provides a common framework of definitions, behavioral descriptions, critical factors, models, and theorems which give the logic designer a deeper understanding of abstract concepts. The designer can use analysis and synthesis techniques to the same extent as he accepts the simplifying assumptions. Flow tables, state transition diagrams, etc. have educational value as descriptive tools. Maley and Earle, in describing some useful sequential circuit designs, use flow table procedures [12]. In a manual on logic circuits, Maley carefully explains the operation of many of the circuits by using Karnaugh maps and flow tables [33]. The flow table also has application outside switching theory; Heistand [34] utilized the concept in constructing an executive control program, and Bredt and McCluskey [35] apply it as a tool to analyze the control of concurrent processes.

As pointed out by Unger, the theory can provide answers to what happens when some assumptions are carried "to the limit" [36]. For example, can circuits be designed that do not malfunction if gate delays could become arbitrarily large? Answers to questions such as these, while not of immediate practical value, can aid the designer's intuition. Theory could also help in the area of categorizing or classifying quantities with which the designers deal. This activity applies to a variety of things, including modes of system timing, delays, hazards, and memory elements.

The theory also plays an important role in activities that are adjunct to the implementation of a digital system. In particular, the study of delays and hazards has not only provided sufficient understanding to avoid malfunctions in circuit designs, but has also provided a basis for simulation programs used for design verification. Present-day machine logic [37] was successfully simulated by applying Eichelberger's ternary analysis [38] developed for fundamental mode circuits. Here, the central clock provides the basic input changes to the logic, and the result of the transition is determined under fundamental mode assumptions. Coding theory has provided a basis for error detection and error correction within digital systems. The subject of testing logic for the purpose of acceptance, as well as for fault location, has benefited greatly from theoretical approaches. Although the theory has provided tests that certify a sequential circuit is operating correctly (machine identification experiments), these tests are quite lengthy. What is required, and what industry is hoping theoretical attacks will provide, are economical test procedures. Elspas states: "Unless much better solutions than are currently available can be found in the next two years, the types and sizes of LSI modules to be fabricated in the future will need to be severely constrained by the lack of adequate test procedures" [1].

Techniques for fault masking or protective redundancy such as triple modular redundancy (TMR), which provide increased system reliability, have followed from the theory and not from ad hoc procedures; various checking schemes have also been provided by theoretical methods. Also, much of the design automation techniques that assist the computer designer are possible because the machine design can be represented abstractly in the computer's file system. In short, the theory can play a supporting role to the computer designer and is of prime importance in many areas adjunct to logic design, such as testing and reliability.

G. Summary and Conclusions

The history of some major fields related to logic design have been traced. The field of logic circuit technology began with relays. Early electronic circuits used both ac-coupled pulse techniques and dc-coupled level-sensitive logic techniques. The dynamic flip-flop inspired the delay line model of a sequential switching circuit. The notion of a logic and timing configuration was introduced, and a large variety of original schemes were employed by the first-generation machine designers. The ambiguity of the term *asynchronous* was shown to have its origin in two of J. H. Bigelow's design concepts for the IAS computer: job completion signaling and dc-coupled level-sensitive gates and flip-flops. Both these principles were points of debate among early logic designers.

As vacuum tube technology gave way to discrete bipolar transistors, dc-coupled clocked systems became more prevalent. With the advent of integrated circuits, capacitive coupling lost favor except for the dynamic MOS FET technology. Interestingly enough, although the technologies have changed, there have developed no logic and timing schemes that were not seen in the first generation.

From the variety of logic and timing schemes emerged mathematical models of sequential switching circuits; in addition, techniques for analysis and synthesis were developed. Caldwell [24] expressed confidence that synthesis techniques such as those that appeared in his book could be adapted to newer technologies. A variety of behavioral descriptive means evolved; these descriptions ranged from the least sophisticated, the timing chart, through the flow table, the transition diagram, the allowed sequence graph, and the regular expression. After the appearance of many timing, memory element delay, and stray delay assumptions and constraints, some attempts were made at classifying the models. The effect of delays and the methods to combat adverse delay distributions were seen to be very important considerations.

In order to better understand the role of logic design, the system design process was reviewed. The symbolic method of logic design was described, and the importance of micro-operations and flow charts stressed. Topics adjunct to logic design—documentation, design languages, simulation, and error control—were covered. The central role of the system timing was brought out, and a classification of logic and timing configurations based upon technological considerations was made. The System/360 Model 50 timing was explained, and some techniques for fitting micro-operations into the machine cycle were discussed.

In the course of tracing historical developments, some interesting controversies, such as the great debate of the Eastern versus Western schools of logic design, were uncovered. In order to understand fully relationships between some concepts that have evolved, a historical approach is necessary. Thus one's understanding of the relationship between "synchronous" and "asynchronous" circuits is incomplete without an appreciation of the roles played by the SEAC and the IAS computer. Many current computers use timing schemes such as multiphased clocks, which coincide neither with the synchronous nor with asynchronous models.

This review of contributions to the fields of logic circuit technology, sequential circuit theory, and logic design practice has placed the reader in a position to appreciate the relationships between these fields. The author's opinions in this matter serve only as a guide, and it is hoped that the reader may now draw his own conclusions on the subject.

In understanding the relationship between logic design practice and sequential machine theory, it is important to recognize the major design problems. The following comment by Hamming, in the context of computer science, has some bearing on logic design: "The engineering aspect is important because most present difficulties in this field do not involve the theoretical question of whether certain things can be done, but rather the practical question of how can they be accomplished well and simply."† In logic design, cost is a critical design factor. Costs can often be minimized by utilizing knowledge of the technology and packaging scheme. Logic design is more closely related to the technology than might be suspected. In logic design practice, the critical design phase is defining a functional unit; however, theoretical sequential machine techniques begin with a well-defined problem statement. In practice, the flow chart and timing chart are

† From R. W. Hamming [23], One Man's View of Computer Science. *J. ACM* **16** (1), pp. 3–12, © January 1969, Association for Computing Machinery. Reprinted by permission.

very important tools, whereas theoretical methods do not use these tools. Also, the designer often "iterates" the design, handling the important circuit inputs and later treating actions required by other input signals which are less important. Theoretical methods unfortunately give all input signals the same status, making problem definitions unwieldy. Internal memory elements in the 1-state often indicate a particular situation exists; whereas in the theoretical state minimization and assignment procedures, certain individual internal state situations that may exist are obscured by the state encoding. With little state assignment encoding, engineering changes are readily handled by modifying the existing circuit; whereas theoretical methods would require the circuit to be redefined as a new problem. The process of debugging involves tracing through logic diagrams in such a way a skill is developed whereby the logic designer is able to view a schematic and determine how it behaves. This ability of the designer to think in terms of the logic blocks themselves and how they are interconnected is then used in generating new designs. For these reasons, many methods of sequential machine theory are not applied directly to computer design. The acceptance of theoretical methods are further complicated by a communication gap between theorists and practitioners. Thus, the author urges the applied researcher to obtain practical experience.

The theory has played a supporting role to logic design; its beginnings were strongly influenced by practice. The theory may dominate in some adjunct areas, such as computer arithmetic, fault masking, coding, and test generation for single faults. The theoretical methods also contribute toward the understanding and classification of types of hazards caused by delays and provide techniques to avoid them. However, some efforts by theorists to classify models have not been useful or illuminating. The reason for this seems to be the great variety of memory element operations and the different levels of observing the circuit operation. Part of the problem lies in the desire of the theorist to economize on the number of models; whereas the engineer must deal with a particular technology and does not need a general model. There is an advantage of having a multiplicity of models available because one can select the one that best fits the problem.

Although a variety of technologies have evolved, the number of logic and timing configurations has essentially remained constant over the last decade. This is seen by Unger as a force for closing the gap; he says: "It seems likely that the gap between theory and practice will diminish, since from a theoretical point of view, many apparently new component and design problems may be analogous to situations encountered earlier".† On

† From S. H. Unger [36], "Asynchronous Sequential Switching Circuits." © 1969, John Wiley & Sons, New York. Reprinted by permission.

the other hand, changes in technology have generally brought about changes in what the engineer would like to minimize in order to achieve an economical design.

A review of the problems of the logic designer over several generations of computers has shown that technology has been the dominant factor. Technology serves as a unifying thread, not only to computer and logic design, but also to the sequential machine models and theory as well.

References

1. B. Elspas, The theory and practice of digital systems. Clearinghouse Rep. AD703747. January 1970. NTIS, Springfield, Virginia 22151.
2. C. C. Foster, "Computer Architecture." Van Nostrand-Reinhold, Princeton, New Jersey, 1970.
3. C. G. Bell, J. Grason, and A. Newell, "Designing Computers and Digital Systems." Digital Press, Maynard, Massachusetts, 1972.
4. T. Kohonen, "Digital Circuits and Devices." Prentice-Hall, Englewood Cliffs, New Jersey, 1972.
5. F. W. Zurcher and B. Randall, Iterative multi-level modeling- A methodology for computer system design. *In* "Information Processing 68" (A. J. H. Morrell, ed.), pp. 867–871. North-Holland Publ., Amsterdam, 1969.
6. D. L. Parnas, More on simulation languages and design methodology for computer systems. *Proc. AFIPS Spring Joint Comput. Conf., Boston, Massachusetts, 1969,* **34,** pp. 739–743. AFIPS Press, Montvale, New Jersey, 1969.
7. Y. Chu, "Digital Computer Design Fundamentals." McGraw-Hill, New York, 1962.
8. D. F. Gorman, Functional design and evaluation. *Proc. AFIPS Fall Joint Comput. Conf., San Francisco, California, 1968,* **33,** pp. 1500–1501. Thompson, Washington, D.C., 1968.
9. M. Phister, "Logical Design of Digital Computers." Wiley, New York, 1958.
10. J. P. Runyan, *IRE Trans. Electron. Comput.* EC-8, 505 (1959).
11. S. Seshu and D. Freeman, The diagnosis of asynchronous sequential switching systems. *IRE Trans. Electron. Comput.* EC-11, 459 (1962).
12. G. A. Maley and J. Earle, "The Logical Design of Transistor Digital Computers." Prentice-Hall, Englewood Cliffs, New Jersey, 1963.
13. E. J. McCluskey, "Introduction to the Theory of Switching Circuits." McGraw-Hill, New York, 1965.
14. H. H. Loomis, Jr., A scheme for synchronizing high-speed logic: Pt. II. *IEEE Trans. Comput.* C-19, 116–123 (1970).
15. S. S. Husson, "Microprogramming: Principles and Practices." Prentice-Hall, Englewood Cliffs, New Jersey, 1970.
16. R. K. Richards, "Arithmetic Operations in Digital Computers." Van Nostrand-Reinhold, Princeton, New Jersey, 1955.
17. R. K. Richards, "Electronic Digital Systems," Chapters 1 and 2. Wiley, New York, 1966.
18. W. E. Donath, Hardware implementation. *Proc. AFIPS Fall Joint Comput. Conf., San Francisco, California, 1968,* **33,** p. 502. Thompson, Washington, D.C., 1968.
19. C. E. Radke, A justification of, and an improvement on, a useful rule for predicting circuit-to-pin ratios. *Proc. Annu. Design Automation Workshop, 6th, Miami Beach, Florida, June 1969,* pp. 257–267. (Available from ACM.)

20. G. W. Schultz, An algorithm for the synthesis of complex sequential networks. *Comput. Design* **8** (3), 49–55 (1969).
21. J. H. Bentley, The foolproof way to sequencer design. *Electron. Design* **21**, 76–81 (1973).
22. D. L. Machart, System timing in a changing design environment. Internal Rep. 07.346, IBM, Rochester, Minnesota, February 13, 1970.
23. R. W. Hamming, One man's view of computer science. *J., Assoc. Comput. Mach.* **16**, 3–12 (1969).
24. S. H. Caldwell, "Switching Circuits and Logical Design." Wiley, New York, 1958.
25. M. H. Mickle, A compiler level program for teaching digital systems design. *IEEE Trans. Educ.* **E-12**, 274–279 (1969).
26. M. C. Woodfill, Teaching digital system design with a minicomputer. *Proc. AFIPS Fall Joint Comput. Conf., 1970,* **37**, pp. 333–342. AFIPS Press, Montvale, New Jersey, 1970.
27. P. Huggins, Universities failing to provide adequate background for DP. *Computerworld,* November 25, 1970, p. 3.
28. W. A. Clark and C. E. Molnar, The promise of macromodular systems. COMPCON 72 Digest, Publ. 72CH0659-3C, pp. 309–312. IEEE, New York, 1972.
29. T. J. Chaney and C. E. Molnar, Anamolous behavior of synchronizer and arbiter circuits. *IEEE Trans. Comput.* **C-22**, 421–422 (1973).
30. Anon., Science and the citizen (Decisions, decisions). *Sci. Amer.* **228** (4), 43–44 (1973).
31. R. McLaughlin, What costs less than $20 and has the compute power of an IBM 704? *Datamation* **15** (11), 198–200 (1969).
32. A. Einstein, "Out of My Later Years." Philosophical Library, New York, 1950.
33. G. A. Maley, "Manual of Logic Circuits." Prentice-Hall, Englewood Cliffs, New Jersey, 1970.
34. R. E. Heistand, An executive system implemented as a finite state machine. *Comm. ACM* **7**, 669–677 (1964).
35. T. H. Bredt and E. J. McCluskey, Analysis and synthesis of control mechanisms for parallel processes. *Symp. Parallel Processor Syst., Technol., and Appli., Naval Postgraduate School, Monterey, California, June 1969.*
36. S. H. Unger, "Asynchronous Sequential Switching Circuits." Wiley, New York, 1969.
37. J. S. Jephson, R. P. McQuarrie, and R. E. Vogelsberg, A three-value computer design verification system. *IBM Syst. J.* **8**, 178–188 (1969).
38. E. B. Eichelberger, Hazard detection in combinational and sequential switching circuits. *IBM J. Res. Develop.* **9**, 90–99 (1965).

Author Index

Pages on which complete references to an author's work are given are printed in *italic*. If an author's work is cited by reference number only, and his name does not appear on that page, the reference number is given in parentheses following the page number.

A

Altman, S. M., 90, *94*
Amdahl, G. M., 41(68), *44*, 98(5), *135*
Anderson, J. P., 106, *136*
Andrews, E. G., 113(75), *138*
Angell, J., 116, *139*
Armstrong, D. B., 55(15), 68, 82, 85, *92, 93, 94*
Astrahan, M. M., 9(14), *42*
Avizienis, A., 114, *138*

B

Bardeen, J., 23(28), *43*
Barnes, G., 38(61), *44*
Bartee, T. C., 74(42), *93, 103, 135*
Bartky, W. S., 61, 84, *92*
Bearnson, L. W., 113(70), 115(70), *138*
Beeson, R. H., 31, *43*
Bell, C. G., 106, 107, *136, 142, 146, 150, 152, 154(3), 155, 161(3), 167*
Bensky, L. S., 98, 99, *135*
Bentley, J. H., 149, *168*
Beter, R. H., 24(34, 35), *43*
Bloch, E., 36, 39, *44*
Boag, T. R., 35, *44*
Booth, T. L., 65, *92*
Bouricius, W. G., 115, 116(93), *139*
Bradley, W. E., 24(34, 35), *43*
Brattain, W. H., 23(28), *43*
Braun, E. L., 131, *140*
Bredt, T. H., 163, *168*
Brooks, F. P., 13, 21, 22, *42*

Brown, R. B., 24(34, 35), *43*
Brown, R. M., 16(21), *42*
Bruno, J., 90, *94*
Buchholz, W., 112, *138*
Burks, A. W., 5(3), *42*

C

Cadden, W. J., 57(19), 59, 74, 76, 77, *92*
Caldwell, S. H., 60, 71, 73, 82, 85, 89, *92, 159, 164, 168*
Camenzind, H. R., 32, 33, *43*
Carter, W. C., 113, 114(85), 115(94), *138, 139*
Case, P. W., 109(51), 117(101), *137, 139*
Chaney, T. J., 161(29), *168*
Chang, H. Y., 111, 114, 115, 116, *137, 138*
Chia, D. K., 116(95), *139*
Chien, K. L., 24(38), 26(38), *43*
Chu, Y., 96, 103, 105, 106, 107, 122, 125, 130, *135, 136, 146, 167*
Clark, W. A., 161(28), *168*
Cole, C. T., Jr., 24(38), 26, *43*
Cole, F. B., 100, *135*
Corning, J., 35(56), *44*
Crozier, J. B., 103(26), *136*

D

Davies, D. C., 32, *43*
Davis, E. M., 35(56), *44*
Dent, J., 115, *138*
Dickinson, M. M., 113(73), *138*
Dietmeyer, D. L., 107, *137*
Dinneen, G. P., 100, *135*
Disson, S., 38(61), *44*

169

Subject Index

174